# IT'S A
# Miracle 2

# IT'S A
# *M*IRACLE 2

MORE INSPIRING
TRUE STORIES BASED ON
THE PAX TV SERIES
"IT'S A MIRACLE"
SELECTED BY

## RICHARD THOMAS

A DELTA TRADE PAPERBACK

IT'S A MIRACLE 2
A Delta Book/April 2003

Published by
Bantam Dell
A Division of Random House, Inc.
New York, New York

Book design by Laurie Jewell

Delta is a registered trademark of Random House, Inc., and the
colophon is a trademark of Random House, Inc.

Library of Congress Cataloging-in-Publication Data
It's a miracle 2 : more inspiring true stories based on the PAX TV
series "It's a miracle"/selected by Richard Thomas.
p.   cm.
ISBN 0-385-33651-9
1. Miracles  I. Thomas, Richard, 1951–  II. It's a miracle
(Television program)

BL487 I44 2003         2002031461
291.4/32 21

Manufactured in the United States of America
Published simultaneously in Canada

BVG   10   9   8   7   6   5   4   3   2   1

# CONTENTS

# INTRODUCTION

I am very happy to be introducing a new volume of miraculous true stories that, I hope, will give you pleasure and inspiration. I'm more convinced than ever of the abiding relevance and impact of narratives that reaffirm the essential worth and dignity of people—stories that tell about the mysterious but undeniable power of our spiritual lives. Many people have been speaking to me about miraculous experiences, and not only the ones they have learned about on our television show, *It's a Miracle*. They tell me about the miracles of their own lives as well. Whether these stories are about healings, separated and reunited loved ones, miraculous escapes from harm's way, or simply about people reaching out and changing each other's lives for the better, they all have the end result of affirming the value of our shared humanity, and they all give us hope.

The world is, as they say, forever changing and forever the same. In the last year, perhaps especially for Americans, life feels different. There is fear and anxiety in the wake of grief and anger. An imagined innocence has been lost; an imagined security has been shattered. But, in important ways, things remain the same. In the midst of disaster, people depended upon and came through for each other in the enduring need for community. We are still looking for happiness and love, inner fulfillment and fellowship, as well as security and success. We still need each other, still reach out to each other, and the stories in this collection are evidence of that. One person helps another. A dream comes true. A second chance is given. The impossible comes to pass. So, no matter how dark the view may be from where we stand, we might try to remember that a miracle is always happening somewhere, and that—just as in these beautiful stories—something wonderful is always possible, for us and for the people we love.

Enjoy!

—RICHARD THOMAS

IT'S A
MIRACLE 2

LOVE FINDS A WAY

# THE ROSENBLATT LOVE STORY

The cruel, inhumane, and unimaginable images of World War II concentration camps remain embedded in our hearts and minds. That *anyone* could have survived these atrocities is a miracle. But Herman Rosenblatt's personal story is especially poignant...and truly miraculous.

Herman was the youngest son in the Rosenblatt family, a loving and happy group of people living in a small village in Poland. But in 1939, the Rosenblatts were forced into a cramped Polish ghetto. Their lives would never be the same. Three years later, Herman's father contracted typhus. It would be the first of many losses for him. And he will never forget what his father said to him on his deathbed.

" 'One thing you've got to remember,' he said. 'Don't hold a grudge against nobody and tolerate everybody.' And the next day, he died."

Germany had taken control of Poland. And four months after his father's death, Herman and his family became victims of Hitler's Final Solution. The ghetto Jews were herded through the streets like cattle, to be transported to their deaths. They were divided into two groups: Herman was to be shipped with the men to a work camp, and his mother was placed with the sick and disabled, to be loaded on a train and sent to the notorious death camp Treblinka.

"I ran over to my mother, and I said, 'I want to be with you. I don't want to go with my brothers,' " recalls Herman. "She went ahead and pushed me away. She said to me, 'Go with your brothers. I don't want you.' Remember, I was at that time twelve years old. I couldn't get over why my mother told me she doesn't want me. She doesn't love me. She went to Treblinka, where she was gassed and died.

"After the war," Herman continues, "I understood why. I still do today. I know why, in my mind, but in my heart, I don't know."

By 1944, Herman was a prisoner in a concentration camp outside Berlin called Schlieben. Life there was a daily struggle under the most horrendous conditions.

"It was hunger, hunger, and hunger," explains Herman. "We didn't get anything to eat. Just one slice of bread and water."

The only escape from constant hunger was in sleep and dreams.

"Once, I was sleeping in the box, and I had a dream that my mother came to me," Herman says, "and she said to me, 'Don't worry, you'll be all right. I'm looking after you.' And she disappeared. And then came an angel who touched me, and she disappeared. And then I woke up in a sweat."

The next day, while Herman was walking near the camp's barbed-wire fence, something caught his eye.

"There was a little girl standing there, looking into the camp," explains Herman. "So I asked her if she had something to eat. And she looked at me. I had the paper suit on and some rags under my feet, and she had a nice, warm jacket, and she took out an apple and threw it. When I caught the apple, I ran away, but I heard her say, 'See you tomorrow.' I believe that the girl who came was the angel my mother was sending to me."

Herman and the young girl continued to meet daily.

"She came every day," Herman says. "Not almost—she came every day. I had it timed when the guards were gonna be in this area and how long it would take another guard to come up, so that when I ran up to the fence to grab the bread or the apple—whatever she threw to me—I wouldn't be seen by the guards. If the SS saw me, I would get shot. But at that point, I didn't care if I got killed or not. As long as I could have some more to eat."

The day came when Herman was to be shipped to another camp, and he said good-bye to the young girl.

"I looked back," Herman remembers, "and she was there. I saw a tear come down her eye, and a tear came down my eye. And I ran away. . . ."

The little girl knew that she would never see him again. When prisoners left this camp, they were often sent to die in the gas chambers.

Nine months later, the Allies liberated the concentration camps. Miraculously, Herman gained his freedom on the very day he was scheduled to be put to death in the gas chamber.

"It was an unbelievable scene," relates Herman. "I couldn't believe it myself. . . . At last, I'm free. . . ."

After spending several years in England and Israel, Herman and his brothers emigrated to the United States and settled in New York City. From 1949 to 1956, Herman was engaged to be married three times, but each time he decided to call it off because he did not feel that he had found his soul mate. And then, in 1957, Herman was invited to join another couple on a date to Coney Island.

"He said, 'But she has a friend of hers who is Polish,'" Herman recalls. "'And we can have a double date.' I replied, 'No, I don't want to go on double dates. Especially blind dates.' He persuaded me, so I said, 'Okay.' She was good-looking. I started to get attracted to her. Eh, I thought to myself, Maybe, maybe after tonight I'll ask her for her telephone number."

Driving home that night, Herman and the young woman, Roma, began talking about their past and discovered that they had actually met once before. It was during his stay in Israel while serving in the Israeli army. One night, he and some fellow soldiers went out with a group of nurses. Roma was one of them.

"She said, 'I had a date with a guy,' and I asked, 'What did he look like?' And she described him to me," recalls Herman, "and I said, 'That was me.' She said, 'Come on. It couldn't be.' I said, 'Yeah.'"

It was an amazing coincidence that these two strangers had met years before. But what was about to happen could only be described as a miracle.

Herman continues, "She said to me, 'Where were you during the war?' I told her, 'I was in a concentration camp.' Then she said to me, 'I was near a camp, where I would throw food over the fences to a boy.'

"I said to her, 'Did he have rags on his feet instead of shoes?' She paused for a second, and then said, 'Yes.' All of a sudden it just hit me like a ton of bricks. I said to her, 'Did he tell you not to come around anymore? That he was leaving?' And she stopped and looked at me."

"Yes," Roma told Herman.

"That was me. That was me," replied Herman. "We paused for a while and didn't say a word to each other. Then I looked at her, and I said, 'Look, you saved my life. You are my angel. And you're going to be my angel.' And I proposed to her."

"He said, 'You know, I'm going to marry you,'" Roma adds. "And I said, 'Crazy . . . we just met. How is this possible?'"

Not only was it possible, it was somehow mysteriously meant to be. Eleven months later, Herman and Roma were wed. The young boy who managed to survive one of the darkest periods in human history, and the angel who risked her life to help him stay alive, were now husband and wife.

And it seemed that nothing could have kept them apart. Not a prison wall, not a separation that would last over twelve years, not even the thousands of miles between a German concentration camp and Coney Island.

"This is destiny," states Roma, "something that I felt very strong. This is the man that God wanted me to have."

Herman and Roma recently celebrated their fortieth wedding anniversary, and they returned to Coney Island to reminisce about that miraculous night when they found each other again.

"Coney Island was the place that we really have special, special feelings about," Roma says. "And I consider myself lucky that we met, and thanks to my friend, and thanks to God, really, that we are together."

"I think that my mother is watching me and she wants me to be happy, and she actually sent Roma to me," Herman concludes. "The miracle was that we kept bumping into each other all the time, and we didn't know it until the last day when we were sitting in the car, and I asked her to marry me. I told her there are no others. . . . There's nobody else for me. And that's it."

IDNEY IN COMMON

Teresa Dravk is a native of York, Pennsylvania. For most of her life, she has suffered from serious heart and kidney problems that have kept her housebound. But in 1997, Teresa discovered the Internet—and it was about to open a whole new world for her.

"I was on there to make friends and to have somebody to talk to," says Teresa. "I wasn't looking for love on the computer—that wasn't something that ever crossed my mind."

Teresa wanted to learn more about life in foreign countries and so, one day, she signed on to a chat room that connected her with people using the Web in Britain.

Thousands of miles away in Manchester, England, Ian Fleming discovered the same on-line site, and he and Teresa started a private chat.

Teresa remembers, "It was the next day when I logged on, and there was this message from the same man—and he had a bunch of questions for me."

"I sent an E-mail to Teresa," Ian recalls, "and it said, 'I like doing my cycling and reading. What do you like doing?' because it was the first person I have ever spoken to on the computer really. She kept it interesting, kept it fun, and explained a lot about her life to me."

The two strangers continued sending each other messages daily.

"And then we found out we had a lot in common, and it just went from there, as far as chatting," says Teresa.

Ian adds, "And it was basically every time I came home from work and did my cycling and walked the dogs, I came in and hoped there was a message from Teresa. I honestly don't know at what point it turned into a romance. It happened and I was glad it happened."

"This was about the time I was starting to get sick with a heart problem," says Teresa.

Teresa's condition was serious and she was immediately scheduled for emergency heart surgery. On the day of the operation, Ian called her at the hospital.

"Well, I told him what was going on and he was very concerned.... I was very scared. You know, at the idea of them doing surgery where they were actually going to stop my heart and open me up."

Ian remembers the conversation. He told Teresa, "Well, I was thinking...I've got time at work that I can take off. Do you want me to come over and visit you? We can spend a couple of weeks together over the holidays."

Teresa was pleasantly surprised. "I said, 'Okay, if you're sure. I'd love to see you.' And every time I heard his voice, it was almost like taking a painkiller. I felt so much better just talking to him."

Teresa's operation was a success. And in December she found herself at the airport, eagerly awaiting the arrival of the man she'd met on the Internet just three months before.

"Teresa walked out into the middle of the crowd and gave me a big hug, and our first kiss. And honestly, from that moment on, I was hooked.... This was the one for me," Ian says.

Teresa recalls, "We just found ourselves connecting more and more on not just superficial subjects like favorite things, but on life issues."

And eleven days later, Ian proposed. Because of Teresa's medical condition, they decided to live in the United States. But before Ian flew home to prepare for the move, they went shopping for an engagement ring. The ring that Teresa chose would have to be resized and would not be ready before Ian's scheduled flight.

On January 6, the young couple said their good-byes. It would be several months before they would see each other again, and during that time, Teresa would become deathly ill. A tumor was discovered on her kidney.

Her doctor, Michael J. Moritz, was extremely concerned.

"Teresa has a rather long medical history as relates to her kidney problems, and she underwent her first kidney transplant in the 1980s, which lasted for quite a while, but ultimately did develop chronic rejection."

The only option now was to remove both her kidneys. Ironically, the day that Teresa was scheduled for the operation was the same day that Ian returned to start their new life together. He had picked up the engagement ring before coming to the hospital, and he took this moment to slip it on the finger of the woman he loved—a woman who might not live much longer if she didn't find a kidney donor.

Teresa remembers, "First, just having him back again after four months, and then to have him put the ring on, knowing what I was going through the next day . . . it was a very, very emotional moment."

Ian wanted to be tested as a donor, but Teresa warned him of the difficulties. She told him, "You know, it's very hard on the donor. And I don't know if I want you to go through that pain."

Ian reasoned, "We're going to be together the rest of our lives, and I'm going to be in pain for only a couple of months, right? At least it will improve the quality of our lives."

Teresa had her doubts. "I really didn't think there was a chance he was going to be a match. I thought we'd go ahead, do the blood test, and that would be it, you know. They'd say, 'Well, I'm sorry, but you're not a match,' and that would be all there was to it."

Says Dr. Moritz, "As you'd expect, for any two unrelated human beings, the odds of being a perfect match in their tissue type is one in three million."

But miraculously, the tests came back positive. They had beaten the incredible odds. Ian was that one person in three million.

On September 19, 1998, Teresa and Ian were married. Their dual surgeries were scheduled two months away. On the morning of November 10, the newlyweds were being simultaneously prepped for transplant surgery at Thomas Jefferson University Hospital in Philadelphia.

Teresa remembers, "We had probably about five minutes where we saw each other."

They wheeled Ian and Teresa past each other and Ian "grabbed hold of Teresa's hand, and said, 'Good luck. See you on the other side.'

"And that was it," Ian says. "That was the last thing I remember."

Teresa says, "I don't really remember what time I woke up, but I woke up in intensive care, and my first question was 'How's Ian? How's he doing?' "

Their surgeries were a complete success, and Teresa and Ian returned to the hospital regularly for checkups. According to Dr. Moritz, "The likelihood of that kidney working a year from now is over ninety-five percent. The chance it will be working ten to fifteen or twenty years from now is better than fifty-fifty."

Says Teresa, "Ian gave me more than just his kidney. He gave me my life back—he gave me self-confidence, courage, self-respect, and self-esteem."

Teresa and Ian's inspirational love story became international news, and the hospital set up a Web page for the couple to receive well wishes from around the world.

Ian recalls, "There were about two hundred messages on there saying 'Good luck, I've been in the same situation.... I've donated a kidney.... I'm on the kidney dialysis.... I know what you're going through....' And I actually cried."

"When we first started talking, not in my wildest dreams would I have ever thought that this was going to be the result of that innocent chat," says Teresa.

Ian agrees, adding, "I really didn't believe in miracles. I always thought that there were explanations to work their way around it. But now, from what I've seen and what I've heard and what I've been through, yeah, there is such a thing as a miracle."

# LOVE AT FIRST SIGHT

The quiet village of Barnstaple, England, is home to Pamela Claypole, who spent thirty-five years working here as an emergency room nurse.

In her free time, Pamela pursued less stressful activities.

"I love gardening, to see the spring flowers come up, the daffodils, the tulips, to see the magnolias blossom," she says.

But the beauty of the world around her was about to disappear.

"I don't know what happened," admits Pamela. "All I can tell you is that I was found here in my house, unconscious."

Pamela had suffered a series of strokes that left her in a

coma, and when she awoke twelve weeks later, her entire world had changed.

"The effects of the strokes were loss of use of my left side, loss of hearing. I couldn't speak for a short time, either," says Pamela. "But within about two days, that came back, and my hearing came back."

What would not return was her near-perfect vision.

"It was as if I lived in a thickness all the time. I couldn't see people's features. All I could see was a misty shape in front of me," she explains. "The doctors examined me and said that I would never see again."

Faced with incurable blindness, Pamela struggled on, slowly learning to navigate her way around her home.

"It was difficult finding my way around to start with, but gradually you come to terms with it," she says.

Still, there were moments of deep despair.

"I sometimes wished that I had not been resuscitated because I felt, without my sight, what is the purpose in life?" she reveals. "I did pray every night—perhaps two or three times during the night, if I woke up—'Please let me see again.'"

Pamela's condition made even the smallest household repairs impossible. Luckily, Mitch Knight, a local handyman, had been recommended by friends.

She called him up, saying, "I hear you're a very good plumber. I've got trouble with my sink. I can't unblock it. Would you come over?"

A single man devoted to his work, Mitch was more than happy to come to the aid of a damsel in distress.

"When I first saw her, she was pretty dismal," recalls Mitch. "She didn't seem very happy. And the eyesight made her feel pretty bad, as if she couldn't do anything."

Mitch had the routine problem fixed within minutes.

"All done," he told her.

"Thank you. How much do I owe you?" she asked.

"No charge," he said. "No charge; I insist. It was a privilege doing it for you."

"I didn't want to put myself out of pocket, but I didn't want to charge her," says Mitch. "I felt something for her. I felt I wanted to help her. I wanted to do this for her." He adds, "And I could see her getting happier, which is what I loved. It made me feel great."

He said to Pamela, "You can be kind one day by making me a cup of tea."

She responded, "Okay, I will. Thank you."

And thus, a friendship was born.

Over the next two years, Mitch would help Pam with both maintenance and gardening, never accepting a penny in payment. At first he helped out for the companionship; later, for something more.

"I had the feeling of love the first time I saw her, and as I kept coming over and seeing her, it got stronger," says Mitch. "I just felt as if I could be with her all my life."

But Mitch was reluctant to share his true feelings with Pamela.

"I think I was afraid, because she didn't know what I looked like," he admits. "She probably wouldn't have the same feelings about me if she could see me."

But all that was about to change. Five years after her stroke, Pamela woke one night, able to see.

"I woke up and I just couldn't believe it, that I could see the clock and other things in the room," she says. "I just sat and cried."

Pamela ran to the front door to look at the world outside.

"I hoped it wasn't going to be temporary," she says. "I thought, This will open up a whole new world to me now. Going out and seeing nature again."

She had to share the incredible news with someone, so she called her best friend Mitch.

"Hello, Mitch . . . it's an emergency! Come quick," she said.

"And he said, 'I'll be right over,'" Pamela recalls. "I just sat here and waited for him to come. I wanted him to share in the joy I had of being able to see."

Because his van was broken down, Mitch ran the half-mile to Pamela's house and arrived in minutes.

"I was afraid that there was water everywhere, or someone was trying to break in, or something like that," says Mitch. "She just said, 'I've got an emergency.'"

Mitch came in through the front door, calling, "Pam, are you okay?"

She told him, "I can see the color of your eyes."

"You can see?" Mitch exclaimed.

"Straight away, I thought a miracle had happened to her. And I felt so happy when this happened that I cried. She felt happy, which was what I wanted," says Mitch.

"When she threw her arms around me, I felt, 'That's it. She can see me and she still likes me.'"

Pamela received a double blessing that night: the return of her sight and recognition of the love of her life.

In January of 1998, Pamela and Mitch were married in a small ceremony with family and friends.

"The love that I feel for Pam is something I'd felt inside me all the time since I'd seen her," says Mitch. "When I got married to her, I just felt, 'We've got a life.'"

Today, Pamela and Mitch are happily married in a relationship in which nothing is ever taken for granted.

"When we do things, when we go out, when we go into town, we're happy," says Mitch.

"I think it happened because of my prayers," Pamela asserts. "I'm a great believer in prayers. All the churches in the area were praying for me too. And obviously, our Lord thought that he would give me the answer to my prayer."

# RESCUE ROMANCE

On January 30, 1983, paramedic Kevin Rolf was on duty in Alachua County, Florida, when an emergency dispatch came through.

"The call came in about a crash of a light plane on take-off, with fire involved and four people inside the plane," recalls Kevin. "Light planes generally don't do very well when they crash, so there's usually severe injuries. The fact that there were four people involved in the plane crash would probably overwhelm the initial responders."

Kevin's instincts were correct. All four passengers had been badly injured.

"When I arrived," Kevin says, "I was given a briefing

on the seriousness of the injuries and a brief rundown on each individual patient."

"One over there has ninety-five percent burns," a paramedic began. "We tried an IV without any luck. We're concentrating on these other ones."

Kevin continues, "I was told that the one that was most critically injured had extensive burns over her entire body. She had been triaged out and they didn't expect that she was going to live."

But something told Kevin to check on her again.

"Ma'am, can you hear me? What's your name?" Kevin asked.

"It's Cheryl," the woman replied.

"I was very surprised to find her awake and responsive," says Kevin. "I had never seen anybody burned as extensively as this woman was, who was still lucid and still aware of her surroundings and still able to communicate."

"All right, I'm gonna get an IV prepped for you. I'm not gonna leave you," Kevin reassured the woman. "I'm right here the whole time."

"My heart went out because I, too, expected that she was going to die soon," he adds. "As a caregiver, I wanted to make sure that she didn't die alone. And that she knew that there were people who cared. That she wasn't by herself. But it was very apparent in talking to her that she wanted to live. And so I wanted to give her that chance."

"Hang in there," Kevin encouraged, "because everything's gonna be okay."

True to his word, Kevin stayed with the young woman until she was transported to the hospital.

"I didn't expect that she would make it to the hospital," Kevin admits. "I fully expected that she probably would die en route. If she did make it to the hospital, she probably would die very shortly after arriving. And I was truly surprised that she was still alive when I walked into the emergency department."

"Take a couple of deep breaths for me," Dr. Layton instructed Cheryl.

"Patients who were burned that severely," Kevin explains, "just didn't survive."

Nurse Joyce Welch was part of the Shands Hospital Burn Team fighting to save Cheryl's life.

"When I first looked at Cheryl," Joyce says, "my opinion of her survival was very slim. Her entire body was completely burned, except for the soles of her feet."

And her injuries were making it impossible for her to tell the doctors something they desperately needed to know.

"Ma'am, are you allergic to anything?" Dr. Layton asked.

"She was very agitated," Kevin remembers, "that nobody seemed to be listening to her. 'Cheryl, this is Kevin,' I told her. And I bent down and asked her, 'What are you trying to tell us?' And that's when she said that she was pregnant and that she couldn't have any X rays, and she couldn't have any drugs."

"Look, we're trying to do everything we can to save her life here, okay," Dr. Layton said.

"Of course they looked at me like I was crazy, didn't I

understand that she was dying and they were just trying to save her life," Kevin adds.

Dr. Joseph Layton was faced with a terrible dilemma.

"Let's get some antibiotics going," he called.

"Cheryl was quite early on, and so there was concern that the drugs that we might have to use could affect a fetus in an adverse manner," explains Dr. Layton. "But we were sort of stuck. The most important issue at that time was to make sure Cheryl didn't die."

The extraordinary efforts of the burn team delivered Cheryl through the critical first twenty-four hours. But saving her three-month-old fetus was beyond their power.

Cheryl's mother, Susanne Kirk, stayed by her daughter's side to give her support through the difficult days ahead.

"Cheryl, it's Mom. We love you so much. You're gonna be fine," Susanne said. She adds, "It was something that we had no control over, and we knew that the baby was lost. It is a mother's worst fear that something horrible will happen to one of her kids. And to have to stand by and be absolutely helpless except for prayer..."

"The doctor said that you're doing really good," Susanne told her daughter. "We love you, sweetheart."

At risk for multiple complications, Cheryl's recovery was by no means certain.

"The doctors informed us that Cheryl would never be able to be a functional person," says Susanne. "That if she was able to leave the hospital, which they greatly doubted, she would not be able to have a full life."

Cheryl's recovery would require months of hospitalization and much more.

"It requires, first of all, a reasonable physiology," Dr. Layton explains. "Cheryl was young and pretty healthy; she had that. It requires an experienced medical nursing team. It requires a determination that will not allow you to give up. Because it's one thing to say 'I'm gonna make it' on day one, but about day 250, it's a little tougher then. And she was determined to pull through all of that, no matter what."

"Walking was very, very difficult for Cheryl," Joyce recalls. "She had to learn how to walk all over again. She had to learn how to use her hands without her fingers. It's kind of like starting all over as a baby. Cheryl basically had to learn all these things all over again."

Part of Cheryl's determination came from the memory of the voice she'd heard at the scene of the accident.

"The first thing I remember," says Cheryl, "was the voice saying, 'Hang in there. Everything's gonna be okay.' The voice was very comforting. Very soothing. The kind of voice that you would expect if you knew what God's voice was.

"My guardian angel told me that everything is gonna be okay and I believed that. And then I'd gone into the emergency room and I started feeling a little anxious about all of these people acting like there was really something bad wrong with me.

"I don't remember hearing the voice again. But I remember feeling this warmth and presence. I could feel him."

And the memory stayed with Cheryl throughout her long and difficult recovery.

"There were a lot of times that I would start getting discouraged or depressed," Cheryl confesses. "But you know, that little voice in the back of my mind kept reflecting on that 'Hang in there. Everything's gonna be okay.'

"I asked a lot of people, and nobody seemed to be able to tell me who the person was who went with the voice," she continues. "After a while, I started believing that it was just a voice that I either imagined or manufactured in my own mind, and that there wasn't really a person who went with the voice."

It would take six more years before Cheryl would learn the truth about the voice she'd heard. And the truth would change her life forever.

Six months after her accident, she was well enough to return home. But her pain was far from over. Shortly after her release, her husband filed for divorce. It was a devastating and emotional blow.

"My feelings were that if the person I had been married to for the last four years wasn't able to accept me, then there was no way I could expect somebody I didn't know to be willing to deal with that," says Cheryl. "I'd pretty much resigned myself to the fact that I was going to be by myself with my animals. I became one of those dog people that didn't have a man in their life. I found that one constant—no matter what happened to me or what I looked like, my animals didn't care. My animals still accepted me for me. They loved me, you know, the way I was. And I think a lot of things that I had to do with dogs were therapeutic for me. I seemed to heal up pretty quick."

Cheryl went on to become a professional breeder and trainer of German Shepherds. After nearly six years and dozens of surgeries, her life was full, active, and happy. . . . But Cheryl had no idea that life was about to deal her another dramatic surprise.

She explains, "I got a phone call from a lady who was looking for a dog for someone who was involved in doing search-and-rescue work. I told her that I did have a dog I thought would be very suitable for that kind of work."

And so she made an appointment to show the dog to the prospective client. It turned out to be none other than Kevin Rolf.

"I recognized her name," says Kevin. "I know there's a lot of Cheryl Bakers. That's a pretty common name. And I really didn't know anything more about her. But it was very obvious that she was a burn survivor. I didn't really say anything to her at the time. We just started talking about the dogs."

"He did like the dog," Cheryl agrees. "The dog liked him. I mean, they were a great pair. As we were filling out the paperwork, he said, 'You know, I gotta tell you, you look a lot better than the last time I saw you.' And I thought, Well, this guy must be crazy, because I don't look very good right now."

"When was that?" asked Cheryl.

"Well, I was at your airplane crash," Kevin told her.

"I'd had a lot of people ask me about the accident, and I didn't mind talking about it," Cheryl continues, "but that's not what he was there for at the time. I was more interested in telling him about the dog and hearing about what he intended to do, search-and-rescue-wise."

"She brushed it off," says Kevin, "and acted like she didn't want to talk about it, which was fine. We didn't need to."

As part of the puppy's sale, Cheryl threw in eight free obedience lessons.

"As we were training the dog over those eight training sessions," Kevin relates, "we enjoyed spending time together; our focus was on the dog, and that was a lot of fun. That started our friendship."

"He was the first person that I'd been around, besides family and friends, that didn't seem to see the scars," Cheryl says. "Didn't care what I looked like. I mean, he was like having a human dog. He treated me like a human being. And it just seemed like we got back more energy than we put into this relationship. We just became really good friends."

"It wasn't until I invited her over for dinner on Mother's Day that it went beyond just training dogs and spending the time working with the dogs," admits Kevin.

"The issue of my accident had never really come up again," Cheryl recalls, "and during dinner I finally asked him, 'What do you remember about it?'"

"Are you sure you want to talk about it?" Kevin asked.

"It was all such a blur to me," Cheryl explains, "that hearing other people's perspectives of it helped me put a lot of pieces together. What did you say to me?"

"I told you just to hang in there, and we'd take care of everything," Kevin replied. He remembers, "This look came over her face. And she just kind of smiled, and she said, 'You're that voice I've been looking for.'"

"I couldn't believe it," Cheryl exclaimed. "I just got really quiet, and I said, 'The day of my accident, what I remember most is someone talking to me, a voice—you're the voice.' That was the point at which I realized that this was the person that went with my little God voice I had remembered all these years. But I didn't want it to change our relationship because now we had this connection."

Cheryl was about to learn that you can't prevent change, especially when it's being guided by love.

"I don't know when I started falling in love with her," Kevin confesses. "I fought being in love or allowing myself to be in love with her for a long while because I didn't want an accident to be the focal part of our relationship. Cheryl knew that, and she kept telling me everything would be okay. Well, I didn't believe her." Kevin laughs. "But I wanted to make certain that it was right. I did not want to have our relationship go bad. I did not want to be the one to hurt Cheryl, ever."

"I did fall in love with him. We had that bond. And I didn't really know how all that was going to play out. But I was willing to see what happened, and I got to like him a lot more than I expected to," laughs Cheryl.

On July 13, 1994, eleven years after the tragic accident that brought them together, Kevin and Cheryl embraced the joy that life had been saving just for them.

"When we decided that we were going to get married, we wanted to get married because we wanted to spend the rest of our lives together," Kevin declares. "And having big weddings and big to-do's and that kind of stuff, it's just not us. So we ran off to Lake Tahoe and got married. Just the two of us."

"We don't have any wedding pictures other than a caricature that was drawn on a boat called the *Tahoe Queen*," Cheryl laughs. "And it kind of reminds me of our whole relationship. We didn't meet the way people normally meet. When we decided to get married, we didn't do it the way people normally do. So for us not to have a wedding picture kind of goes along with it. I love the wedding picture that we have. You know, it just fits us."

Today, nearly twenty years after their miraculous meeting, the love that brought Kevin and Cheryl together continues.

"Kevin's love for me has changed my whole life," concludes Cheryl, "because I didn't think somebody could love me. He's my whole world. Everything that I have...I could live without...except him. He means more than the world to me."

"I love her with all my heart," Kevin concurs. "She's my soul. She's everything good that happens in my life. It's definitely a miracle that she survived and left the burn unit, then went home and was able to make her recovery. And then the miracle that we were reunited. It was a miracle that Cheryl didn't just brush me aside when I brought up her accident and she didn't want to talk about it. But every day is a miracle, because we have it to share together. And I'm really looking forward to the rest of my life."

# $\mathcal{A}$FFAIR OF THE HEART

In October 1994, Eppie Simpson was diagnosed with a rare genetic heart disorder. Over the next two years, this once active woman would undergo hundreds of procedures to save her life, including seventeen heart catheterizations. The operations left her weak, her spirit depleted. And then in 1996, Eppie's heart was broken. Her husband died unexpectedly, and, in her grief, she suffered a massive heart attack. From that point on, she was in constant pain, enduring two bypass operations and living on painkillers and other drugs.

By the time she arrived at the cardiovascular research center at Johns Hopkins Hospital, under the care of Dr. Jon

Resar, Eppie was desperate. But there was very little hope that her condition would improve.

Dr. Resar remembers, "Eppie had frequent episodes of chest pain, really with very minimal activity, and often at rest. So as you could imagine, this type of constant chest pain is severely disabling, preventing her from doing any of the normal activities you and I would routinely perform."

The only option left for Eppie was a dangerous, experimental surgery using lasers to drill new channels in her heart to improve her blood flow—and hopefully to save her life.

Research coordinator Kathy Citro explains, "Eppie was a perfect candidate for this study. She was young, otherwise healthy, had had two previous bypass surgeries and multiple angioplasties, and she was also very interested in doing whatever she could to improve her lifestyle."

At the same time, another heart patient was looking for a miracle in his life. Harold Carmical had also suffered a massive heart attack and, during emergency surgery, a balloon used to open his artery burst because of extreme calcium blockage. Harold was put on a diet of nitroglycerin pills. Normal heart surgery was out of the question.

"Harold was in a very similar position to Eppie," says Dr. Resar. "They had been hospitalized, they had had numerous procedures, and they were unable to do their daily activities."

Luckily, Harold also qualified for the experimental procedure.

Kathy Citro remembers, "I told Harold that there was

another person in the program, and that the two of them would be going through the process at about the same time. I thought it would be a good idea for them to get through this process together, because it was new; it had never been done before at Hopkins. It was pretty frightening, really, when you think that they're going to drill channels in a person's heart with a laser. So I thought it would be a good idea for them to get through this together."

The two heart patients agreed to meet in the coffee shop of a local hotel.

Eppie recalls, "I was nervous, and I'm a very shy person. I thought he was a kind man. He was very easy to talk to. And he made you not feel nervous. I liked his personality. I sat back and listened."

What Eppie learned was that Harold was also suffering from the loss of a relationship. His life had become a series of stressful, painful, and lonely days. And now he was facing a delicate untested surgery.

Harold remembers thinking, I'd been through a lot of things; I really didn't have any choice. I knew that I couldn't go on like I was living.

This brief meeting between two strangers, each with only one slim hope to live, would be the start of a miracle.

The next day, both Harold and Eppie underwent surgery. Each of their operations lasted over six hours, but amazingly they both survived this dangerous, experimental procedure. Barring any complications, they were sent home to recuperate—Eppie to Delaware, Harold to Kentucky. But their bond continued to grow as they spoke to each other nightly.

"We were two people who had the same thing in common," says Harold. "She'd call me about her problems, and I would talk to her, and it went from there."

"I was starting to feel different feelings for Harold at that time," says Eppie. "It was a relief to have somebody else to talk to."

Four months later, Harold made an important decision.

"Harold decided to come and visit in March, but before he came to visit, he sent me a dozen red roses with one white rose in the center, which means, 'I love you.' And that made me nervous," Eppie recalls with a laugh. "Then I was like, Okay, I haven't dated in twenty years now!

"So we pulled into a parking lot and we started talking, and very shortly, he kissed me. And that's what I wanted! I was very nervous—I was like a kid again. I haven't done that in a long time. One kiss, and I knew I was falling in love with him. I knew we were going to be together."

Eppie and Harold returned to Johns Hopkins for their routine six-month checkup—which turned out to be anything but routine. Harold surprised Eppie with a heart-shaped engagement ring and a proposal of marriage.

Kathy Citro remembers, "Harold just pulled out this ring and gave it to Eppie right there in front of all of us working in the lab, and it was very exciting. Eppie was absolutely thrilled by it."

"He gave me the ring," Eppie recalls happily, "and he asked me if I would marry him, and I said, 'Yes.' I said yes several times."

Dr. Resar had a hunch. "I had a suspicion that there was a romance developing between the two. I was, in fact, so suspicious that I actually mentioned to Kathy that I thought there was a blossoming romance, and she scoffed at me and said, 'No, I don't think so.' "

"I was really thrilled to see how it evolved into this romantic relationship, and the two of them really, really seem to be made for each other," Kathy says.

Even though they each had vowed never to remarry, Eppie and Harold were wed just two and a half months later. Miraculously, what started as a cure for their diseased hearts ended up fixing their broken hearts as well.

Kathy adds, "They have not only improved their health, but they've found life partners—and to me, that's a miracle."

"The best thing that happened to me since this procedure is Harold Carmical," concludes Eppie. "Because we're meant for each other, and we have new hearts, and we're going to conquer many things together."

# HEAVEN SENT

The personal ads. They contain thousands of stories of lonely people looking for love—and at least one story that could be a miracle. It all began in 1973 with a dream: a vision of a mysterious red-haired lady seated at a church organ. The dreamer was Kris Henry, a young woman living in St. Petersburg, Florida.

The woman in Kris's dream spoke very clearly to her, saying, "I want you to place a personal ad." The woman went on to tell Kris exactly what it should say. Although the words of the woman in the dream made no sense, Kris was compelled to write them down when she awakened.

The next day, Kris's employer, Doris, saw the note and

asked Kris about it. Kris explains, "I said, 'It was just a dream with this lady. She was telling me to write this ad and to publish it in a paper. It was just a dream; don't worry about it.'"

But Kris's boss took matters into her own hands and sent the note to the local classifieds.

A few nights later, the persistent figure returned to Kris's dreams. This time, her message was even more specific. The red-haired woman told Kris, "Respond only to the typewritten letter."

The next day, Kris told her boss about the second encounter. "I said, 'Guess what?'" Kris recalls. "'I had another dream about that pretty lady with the red hair in front of the organ. She told me to only respond to the typewritten letter.' And Doris started laughing, because she said, 'Well, I put it in the publication.'"

Two weeks later, a large envelope arrived with over sixty-five responses to the personal ad. To Kris's amazement, there was only one typewritten letter. It was from Jim Kelley.

Jim says, "I actually wrote it out first and then I typed it as well. It looked more professional and with those types of columns, you're kind of leery anyway. If it comes in as a typed letter, you possibly have a chance and that person will talk to you. So that's what I did."

After several telephone conversations, Kris and Jim finally made a date to go dancing at a country-western bar.

"When I first saw her," Jim remembers, "she was so beautiful, and I said to myself, Well, this will be a one-shot date, because I'm not gonna be able to compete with this."

Kris says, "When I saw him, he was the most romantic-looking man I'd ever seen in my life."

Jim felt that "there was something there. It was almost like a spiritual connection, because everything just clicked, almost like a soul mate-type situation. You had found somebody you were very attracted to."

And Kris agrees. "If he had said, 'Do you want to marry me?' I would have said, 'Yes!' right then and there. That's how I felt."

Kris and Jim fell deeply in love and were married three years later. The newlywed couple was very aware that a miraculous sequence of events had brought them together. But there is one more incredible event in their story.

While visiting Jim's mother, Kris paged through a family album, when she noticed a photograph that took her breath away.

Says Kris, "There was the woman with the red hair looking right at me. And I said, 'That's her; that's the lady in my dream! She's the one that told me what to say.' "

Another photograph showed the same woman standing next to Jim. Kris was shocked and asked Jim who she was.

Jim recalls, "I became very emotional. I said, 'That's my wife who died of cancer.' "

Unknown to Kris, Jim's first wife, Georgia, had lost a difficult battle with cancer, and Jim had been silently mourning her loss. Jim explains, "In Kris's dream, when she had mentioned that she saw the woman sitting at an organ, that was a kind of confirmation for me in my own thoughts, because Georgia used to play a church organ."

Kris felt an immediate connection to Jim's deceased

wife. "The love I had for this woman..." Kris says, "It was an honor to be directed and led by her, and to be picked by her to be with Jim."

Both Jim and Kris were convinced that her dreams were a message of love and proof that miracles do happen.

Says Jim, "I think this happened because Georgia basically wanted me to continue on in a relationship, and not just be wandering in the desert like the nomads."

And Kris speculates, "I guess she knew that I would be his best friend. I would take care of him and make sure that he was loved, and that's all he'd ever know."

Jim is convinced that "this story definitely is a miracle. It demonstrates that love goes beyond the grave; it still continues."

"Her influence has been with us all these years," reflects Kris. "They had a very special marriage. To know that I'm handpicked by that spirit, you can't get any better than that."

# OVERCOMING THE ODDS

# SARAH'S STORY

"When Sarah was a really little girl, she was always mischievous; one who loved to get a prank over on you," says her mother, Cleta Dell'antonia. "Her thing when she was real tiny was, she loved to scare you."

And on a spring day in 1988, little Sarah managed to scare her mother so intensely that Cleta will be haunted by what happened for the rest of her life.

"My husband had told us that when he got off work that evening, we would go out to the park to play, but he was gonna mow the lawn first," recalls Cleta. "So I told the kids that instead of waiting for Daddy to get home, we would have more time at the park if I went ahead and mowed. The kids thought this was great."

Cleta brought out the riding lawn mower and told four-year-old Sarah to play on the porch.

But true to her nature, Sarah decided to frighten her mother by running directly into the path of the mower: an act that would set off a terrifying chain of events.

"I heard this noise, and I thought that I'd hit a stick and it just kept clattering. I thought, Well, the stick must've gotten wound up in there," says Cleta. "And then I saw Sarah laying over on the ground."

Cleta rushed to her daughter's side.

"I saw she had blood on her, and I couldn't imagine why. I realized at this point that it was actually my daughter that I had hit with the mower. I began wiping her legs off, and I saw that there were no feet on her. And she was bleeding so bad, I didn't think she would live."

With no time to lose, Cleta grabbed her daughter and raced to her car, driving Sarah to the hospital on her own.

"I held both her legs, often with only one hand, trying to keep the bleeding down," says Cleta. "And when we got about halfway to the hospital, she rolled these big blue eyes of hers up at me, and she just said, 'Mommy, am I gonna die?' And it was really hard for me to tell her, 'No, you're not going to die,' because in my own heart, I knew there was a good chance that she might die."

Minutes later they arrived at Mercy Hospital, and once inside, the emergency room staff worked feverishly to stabilize Sarah's condition.

"I knew she was hurt bad, but I was wanting to go in and just have the doctors say, 'Cleta, she's hurt, but she's not hurt as bad as you think,'" confesses Cleta. "That wasn't the case."

The doctors told Cleta that Sarah's injuries were so severe that she would have to be life-flighted to Kansas University Medical Center in Kansas City. Cleta called her husband, Bill, with the tragic news. He raced to the hospital, afraid of what he might find.

"When I first saw her laying there, the first thing that came was, 'Why, Lord, why does it have to happen to a four-year-old?'" says Bill. "The doctors told me that her feet had been chopped off clean, completely. I was in total shock."

At Kansas University Medical Center, Sarah underwent immediate surgery.

"And I was sitting there, wondering, Why aren't they coming out here and telling me something?" says Cleta. "And I prayed so much, 'Just let this child live' and 'Please let her be a kid again.'"

In a grueling eighteen-hour surgery, the doctors attempted an innovative procedure to avoid amputating Sarah's legs below the knees. By taking muscle from her back and transferring it to her damaged limbs, they were able to salvage Sarah's ankles and heels.

"When the doctor came out of the surgery room, he had such a solemn look on his face," recalls Cleta, "I knew that the news wasn't gonna be good. He told us—I will never forget it—he looked at Bill and me and he goes, 'I don't think your daughter will ever walk again.' I thought, My God, she's only four years old."

"It was scary. We had a little girl sitting here that previously could walk, and now she can't walk, and now what are we going to do?" says Bill. "Will she ever be able to walk again?"

Only Sarah could answer that question. After a month in the hospital, this brave young girl was back at home, determined to prove the doctors wrong.

"I carried her into the bathroom," remembers Cleta, "and she came out, just screaming, 'Mama, come here, come here.' So I went in, thinking, What's wrong? When I got there, she says, 'I can walk, Mama.' I just broke down and cried, and I said, 'Sarah, you can't walk.'"

"Mommy, I can walk," said Sarah.

"And it was bad, but she was walking," says Cleta.

"I was so proud of her that day, I just about couldn't stand it," recalls Bill. "She's sitting on the floor, looking up at me like, 'Who cares, Dad? I don't care if I was injured. There's nobody gonna stop me from walking. I still have feet.'"

The road to recovery was long and painful, but Sarah refused to give up. Just six months after her accident, the doctor said that she was ready to try prosthetics.

"At that time, they had these real tall fiberglass prosthetics, and they weighed more than she did," says Cleta. "She would cry, and she would tell me, 'Mommy, they hurt so bad, I don't want to wear my'—she called them 'boots'—'I don't want to wear my boots, Mommy.'"

"I didn't want this girl ruined," says Bill. "This girl is energetic; she's determined to walk. I don't care if I have to go to the ends of the earth, I need to find somebody who can come up with an innovative idea."

And the Dell'antonias found that somebody. His name was Doyle Black, of Hanger Prosthetics and Orthotics.

"I felt that Sarah was a little girl that needed all the help she could get," says Doyle. "I was willing to go that extra mile to make sure that she got what she needed."

"Doyle told us, at this point, that he had an idea for a silicone prosthetic," recalls Bill.

"Silicone was a new challenge to us because, at that time, a silicone foot had never been made," explains Doyle. "There was no better reason for us to try it than when Sarah came in."

Using a special substance called alginate, Doyle cast a mold of Sarah's remaining limbs. It was from this mold that he created a very special pair of silicone feet.

"When I brought the prostheses in to her, her eyes got as big as silver dollars, and she looked at dad and she looked at mom, and just grinned. She said, 'Mom, I like these. I want these, Mom. Can I have these, Mom?'" remembers Doyle, laughing.

"When he first got the prosthetics done and she put them on, it did as much for her ego, I think, as it did mine," says Cleta, "'cause she would say, 'Mommy, I can run in my feet, Mommy, look at my feet.' She never called them boots. She actually called them feet."

"It was very touching that we were able to give her back what was taken away from her," says Doyle.

Over the years, Sarah has returned to Doyle each time she grew, to get new feet. And as a teenager, she's been able to adapt to life like any other sixteen-year-old.

"There's not anything I can't do with my feet," says Sarah. "I mean, I run, I jog, I ride a bike, I do everything. There's not really anything I can't do."

"I was really worried about the boyfriends, you know, if she would have boyfriends or not," confesses her mother. "And now it's been quite the opposite. The phone rings too often, in my estimation."

"I date as many guys as anybody else, if not more," says Sarah. "No, I'm kidding."

Like other girls her age, Sarah had a dream . . . but it would be a difficult mountain to climb.

"I've always wanted to be a cheerleader, since I was little bitty," reveals Sarah. "Even when I was little, every year for Halloween I'd be a cheerleader, you know?"

"When Sarah announced that she really wanted to become a cheerleader, and she was gonna try out, we were shocked," says her father. "I was really concerned at that point. She walks, yeah, she runs, yes, but can she really do all the jumps? Can she really compete with somebody at that point?"

"I went ahead and tried out and I was really nervous, 'cause there's a lot of people that try out," recalls Sarah.

Her mother was with her on the day they announced who had qualified.

"Sarah was really crying, and I looked at her, and I put my arm around her. I said, 'Sarah, it's okay,'" says Cleta, "and she says, 'Mama, I'm crying because I made it. I'm crying because I'm happy. I'm a cheerleader, Mom; I'm finally a cheerleader.'"

"The first time I saw Sarah cheerleading, it choked me up," her father says. "I could not believe that Daddy's little girl was out there cheerleading. She was bouncing; she was running up and down the court. We could not tell the difference between Sarah and the other cheerleaders. Sarah was just Sarah. I mean, she was one of the girls. She was part of the action. There she was. It's just a feeling you can't describe when you see a girl that you've come so far with. It's breathtaking.

"These feet have actually helped me to start to believe that there must be a power somewhere. These feet came from God, the idea did, but Doyle Black, perhaps through God, worked a miracle."

"When I see Sarah at the games, I am so proud of her," says Cleta. "All of her accomplishments and everything that she has done. There's a part of me that just wants to stand up and scream to the crowd, 'That's my daughter.'"

# FOOTBALL COACH

If a miracle is something that defies odds—that overcomes insurmountable obstacles to achieve the impossible—then Jeffrey Pontius is a living example. Jeffrey is a twenty-one-year-old college student who has chosen a career that most people cannot begin to accept or understand, given his physical limitations.

Jeffrey was born with cerebral palsy, a disease that left him nearly quadriplegic. His grandparents, Elsie and Wayne Trick, raised him on the outskirts of Seattle, Washington.

"Jeffrey was very limited in his abilities," recalls Elsie. "He could not walk. His speech was unintelligible, he was spastic, and so he had jerky movements."

But she adds, "From the very beginning, when I looked

into Jeffrey's eyes, I knew he was intelligent. I knew that there was something in there that was more pronounced than his physical limitations."

When he was old enough to be tested, it was discovered that Jeffrey's IQ was way above normal, approaching genius. And he proved it by excelling at school, always staying at the top of his class.

"Jeffrey was always a positive person, and there was no holding him back on anything he wanted to do," says Wayne. "If he would try something new, he would stay with it for hours until he succeeded in doing what he wanted to do."

And then when he was eleven, Jeffrey witnessed an event that would change the course of his life: a football game.

"Watching that football game ignited something inside of Jeffrey," Elsie says. "And he was never the same about football. He just yelled and whooped and hollered. He just moved his arms and his feet and thoroughly enjoyed it."

At that moment, Jeffrey made a decision: He was going to become an athlete.

"It was an outlet for his being so competitive," says his grandmother, "because he is. I think he's the most competitive person I've ever seen, in anything he does."

During the next three years, Jeffrey won ten first-place ribbons at the Washington State games for the disabled.

"I felt that the only way I could prove myself to be the best at anything was to go out and win something," admits Jeffrey.

It was during this time that Jeffrey gained a voice

through a computer-driven device called—appropriately—a liberator.

"It's my way to communicate, plain and simple," he says.

"His wrist, the way it curves down due to cerebral palsy, makes it just right where he can use that finger to type," says Wayne.

Jeffrey programmed the device himself, ensuring that every word and phrase was tailored to his needs.

"Basically, there are about 10,000 words and phrases programmed under different combinations of buttons. Without this, it would take much longer to communicate with people," Jeffrey explains.

And what does he like to talk about most? Football.

"What I like about football is that it involves a lot of strategy and preparation," he says.

And so Jeffrey decided to follow his heart, and work to become a professional football coach. His career counselors were less than enthusiastic.

"The people did not know how to react to my dream, and they were speechless," Jeffrey recalls. "If I were in their situation, who knows how I would have reacted."

But Jeffrey wasn't giving up. When he entered the University of Missouri in 1996, even before registering for classes, he headed for the football field to meet Larry Smith, coach of the Missouri Tigers.

"I was just completely enthralled with his presentation and his personality," says Larry. "He let it be known that someday he was seriously thinking about...that he would like to try to be a football coach. That began the relationship, I think, right there with the team."

Impressed with Jeffrey's determination and knowledge of the game, Coach Smith gave him a chance to prove himself.

"I started just by watching practices my first year," says Jeffrey. "After that season, I started coming to more practices, meetings, and my role as a coach has slowly expanded."

Jeffrey attends every football practice and home game. The more football he sees, the more he wants to coach.

"I think he has a pretty good understanding of what it takes to play the game, and what can be successful and what can't be," maintains Larry.

He often meets with the coaching staff to help analyze game videos. Associate Head Coach Ricky Hunley relies on Jeffrey's unique perspective of the game.

"He's got a great eye," says Ricky. "He watches every game, and I give him a grade sheet and he grades the players in his own mind. He keeps a running log of all the defenses, all the checks, all the adjustments.

"He's an incredible person. You know, he has so much energy and wisdom. And he is just an inspiration to my players," Ricky adds.

Defensive coordinator Moe Ankney finds Jeffrey inspiring as well.

"His attitude about everything is so good that I don't think there's anything that he can't accomplish when he puts his mind to it," declares Moe. "He has, over the course of the years that he's been here, given some of the best motivational speeches and talks to our players of any of our coaches."

"Being disabled, you learn how to cope with challenges, and I pass these lessons on to the team," says Jeffrey.

Jeffrey's goal has become very specific. Within ten years, he plans to become coach of the Missouri Tigers.

"He is a regular, normal person," says Coach Larry Smith. "And all he thinks about is what he wants to get done, so I think from that standpoint, his perseverance and his determination are going to take him a long way."

Those who know him say that Jeffrey's goal is not unrealistic. They see many miracles in his life.

"I think Jeffrey Pontius is a miracle in itself," says Ricky Hunley. "I wish I had what he has inside."

# DESERTED BABY VALEDICTORIAN

In 1982, a newborn boy was abandoned at the door of a Los Angeles hospital. There was no note, no explanation, just an innocent child left to fend for himself. As you are about to read, it's going to take a miracle and the love of dedicated parents for this child to survive, for he was born addicted to crack cocaine. The infant was going through severe withdrawal and would most likely suffer severe brain damage. Forsaken, weak, with no one to care for him, the obstacles this infant faced seemed insurmountable.

Dr. Mitchell Goldstein, a staff neonatologist at Providence St. Joseph Hospital in Burbank, California, explains the syndrome. "With these babies who have had cocaine exposure, they're born without the ability to really direct attention, without the ability to really focus on what is normal newborn function. They are unable to really get attached to the mother and the father and essentially experience what it is to be a newborn."

To provide foster care for the infant, the Los Angeles County Child Welfare Agency contacted Ila and Dale Pawley, veteran foster parents.

Dale says, "We weren't concerned about having a drug-addicted baby, because we really didn't know what it involved."

Ila continues, "We went into it with our eyes open, with no reservations, no preconceived ideas. We just knew that this child needed a home, he was very sick, and he needed someone to love him."

The Pawleys named the baby Dale Daniel, D.D. for short. Although they had no previous experience caring for drug-addicted infants, what they lacked in professional expertise, they made up for in love.

"The first day and night that we had him," Ila remembers, "he cried continually. He flailed about; he was unable to relax. The cry of a drug-addicted baby is so much different from a regular, normal baby. It's almost a piercing, urgent, frightening cry that they have, and it's because they're in pain; they're withdrawing from drugs. And so we tried to keep him calm, and rocking him seemed to calm him."

The Pawleys' first days with D.D. were filled with tension. In spite of their best efforts, D.D. was unable to develop any regular sleep patterns and was suffering from severe sleep deprivation.

Ila describes the difficulties they faced. "The prognosis at first with D.D. was, we were told so many times over and over, 'Well, you're wasting your time. He's not going to really develop normally, he will have problems all of his life.'"

But the Pawleys saw something special in D.D. that doctors could not. When D.D. was two years old, Ila and Dale legally adopted their foster son.

Dale says, "We did not accept anyone's prognosis that he was not going to be totally normal the rest of his life. We knew that there was a real spark in him. So we tried to develop that."

Slowly, painstakingly, little D.D. began to show signs of recovery. But for every step forward, there were two steps back.

Says Ila, "He loved kindergarten, but he would inappropriately get up and walk around the room, or twirl, or decide that he was going to talk continually then, and disrupt the entire school. The teachers were not able to cope with it."

When it was obvious that D.D. could not function in a normal school environment, the Pawleys took on an even more difficult task. They chose to homeschool their son.

"I began to teach him," Ila explains, "and I realized he was learning very rapidly. But he was able to stimulate himself with the twirling and the rocking in between. When he wasn't doing it, I was able to get through to him, to teach him, and he retained it."

As D.D. entered his middle school years, his ability to learn increased rapidly. Still under his parents' homeschool tutoring, D.D. made a remarkable decision. He told his parents that he wanted to finish high school two years early.

At first, Ila was worried. "When he decided that he was going to double up on his courses, there were many times I said to my husband, 'He'll never make it. This is too much of a challenge; it's too hard of a job.'"

Dale recalls, "He didn't listen to people when they said he was going to fail. And that's the way he's going to be through his whole life."

Day after day, hour after hour, D.D. pored over English, math, history, and science courses. With every step, his parents were by his side, encouraging him and praying for him.

Says Ila, "D.D. is very special, and he has high ideals. He's expressed it to us and to other people, too, that he's going to really do something special. And I believe he is."

In June of 1998, D.D. Pawley proved to the world that he was capable of meeting the challenge. At age sixteen, he graduated from high school as valedictorian of his homeschool group. The next year, D.D. would attend college.

At D.D.'s graduation ceremony, Ila said, "It's really rewarding to me as a teacher to see him tonight, standing up there to give his speech, and I'm just very, very proud." At the ceremony, D.D. said, "I would like to thank my mother, Ila Pawley. Thank you and God bless you."

Dr. Goldstein says of D.D.'s accomplishments, "What has gone on with D.D. Pawley is truly amazing, where a child has overcome the disadvantage, essentially, of a drug addiction at birth, and gone on to succeed despite this. The miracle here is that this child has done so well despite society. You really don't see this. This is truly unique."

For D.D., Ila, and Dale Pawley, the dramatic turnaround of D.D.'s life is nothing short of a miracle.

D.D. certainly thinks so. "The miracle for me here is that someone who could have ended up in such a bad place—the ghetto, maybe being on drugs, in gangs and stuff—could end up the way I am, graduating two years early, with great parents like mine."

Ila says, "I just love him so much and I'm so proud of him. I'm proud of everything the kids have accomplished here, all the kids, but especially my son."

And Dan agrees. "Miracles can happen when people believe, whether the miracle be from something spiritual, or from within yourself. D.D. made himself, and may have generated the miracle by defying all the odds."

# DAUGHTER SHOT

It was Thanksgiving Day 1988, and Bertha Burns was preparing her annual feast for friends and family. Her two young daughters, Cheryl and Maryann, had gone across the street to play with some neighborhood children before the guests arrived.

Although Bertha had only met her neighbors a few times, she knew the girls were all friends at school and felt comfortable knowing they were just a few doors away. But today, the children were not getting along, and Cheryl and another little girl began quarreling.

Cheryl remembers, "Me and the other little girl got into a little argument, a little kid argument, saying, 'My dad could beat up your dad.' And she was like, 'My dad could beat up your dad, 'cause my dad has a gun.' "

Cheryl didn't believe the little girl, so now she was going to prove that her father's gun was real. She entered her parents' bedroom and opened a box that she'd been told never to touch. Then she took the loaded gun back outside.

"When she came out with the gun, I was surprised, because I didn't think she really had one," explains Cheryl. "I was just staring at it, and then I told my sister, 'Let's go.' "

But before she could convince her sister to leave, tragedy struck. The bullet entered Maryann through the back of her head.

"I felt like passing out," says Cheryl. "I just remember, I mean, I turned cold. I just ran to my mom."

Bertha raced to her daughter's side, but her tiny body was limp and lifeless. She instinctively knew that if she waited for an ambulance, Maryann might not survive.

"I didn't stop to call 911," remembers Bertha. "I just picked up my daughter, even though she was bleeding a lot."

Bertha's cousin, Rubin, had just arrived for Thanksgiving dinner and drove them to the hospital. Minutes later, Bertha arrived at the emergency admitting room, still clutching her child in her arms.

"There was a man there dressed in white, and he was the one I handed her to," Bertha recalls.

Maryann was rushed to a trauma center for emergency surgery. The bullet had shattered into five pieces upon entering the child's skull. Surgeons worked frantically to remove the fragments from her brain, any one of which could prove fatal. Several hours later, Bertha finally learned the condition of her child.

"They told me they already operated and gave her blood, but she was in a coma," says Bertha.

Dr. Paa, a member of the surgical team, explains the dangers involved. "When the child is unconscious, being kept under immediately after surgery, we have no way of assessing what condition we're going to find when she wakes up. We were very worried that she would have a major neurological deficit—a permanent one."

Bertha remembers, "He told me about the consequences she might suffer. That she wouldn't be the same normal girl. I started asking God with all my heart—crying and everything—'Dear God, give my daughter back the way she was.'"

Maryann's father, Jim Burns, had been out of town and arrived at the hospital around midnight. He was not prepared for what he found there.

"I was devastated, at a loss for words, shocked—and then I just wanted to be there for her," Jim remembers.

Jim and Bertha took turns staying by Maryann's bedside day and night.

"I always talked to her and told her, 'No matter what happens, we'll always be there for you,'" says Jim.

By now, Maryann had remained in a coma for several days and her doctors were worried she might never regain consciousness.

"I never stopped praying for her," Bertha recalls. "I never stopped asking God to save my daughter."

Maryann's parents were concerned about letting her sister Cheryl see her in the condition that she was in, but after days of Cheryl's pleading, they finally relented.

"I thought that she was dead," Cheryl remembers. "I thought that she wasn't there, because she wasn't moving. It was really hard, because she was attached to all these tubes and I just wanted to take them out so we could play hide-and-seek."

Cheryl joined the vigil by her sister's side. And the next day, the family's prayers were answered. Maryann regained consciousness. But even though she was conscious, doctors warned the family that Maryann would most likely be paralyzed and suffer brain damage, including loss of vision and speech.

But the very next day, another miracle occurred. Maryann was sitting up in bed and talking to her family. Still, the doctors remained skeptical as to whether she would ever walk again. But whatever power was watching over little Maryann, it continued to work, and two and a half weeks after being shot in the head, she was walking and running like a normal child.

"The miracle here is that she wasn't destroyed by that gunshot wound," says Dr. Paa. "A .38 caliber weapon is a major wound. The miracle is that you can be shot in the head with a police caliber weapon and come out of it with a little clumsiness in your one hand and nothing more."

Today, at the age of twelve, Maryann is completely recovered and has returned to the San Diego Children's Hospital to receive a special award for her courage.

A doctor addresses the audience: "It's ten years later, she's a miracle story, and she's a testament to the commitment and prayers and spiritual beliefs of a number of people."

Then it's Maryann's turn to speak. "Hi, my name is Maryann Burns, and I was shot in my head, and it almost ended my life. But thanks to God, I am alive today."

Says Jim, "I think everybody's here for a reason, and I don't think her fulfillment to society was done. So that's where it becomes a miracle."

Bertha adds, "I am very proud of her. I prayed, I had faith, believing that she would be fine, and she was given back to me. It is a miracle."

# $\mathcal{E}$YE-OPENING SIGHT

When Amy Pitchforth was just four months old, her mother, Sharon, discovered that she was suffering from a disturbing condition.

Sharon says, "Pretty much since she was born, I noticed that her eyes would constantly wiggle. It was a real concern, so I took her to her primary doctor at that time."

His examination uncovered a coloboma, or severe gap, that affected the development of her retina and optic nerve.

Dr. Keith Burkart was Amy's optometrist. "A child that is born with a coloboma," he explains, "will not have any vision in the area where the coloboma occurs. This condition reaches a certain point where it stops and doesn't get worse, but it doesn't get better."

Sharon says, "When they told us that she would never see very well, we figured that what we'd do is just let her do everything and anything she wanted, so that she'd have a normal childhood."

But normal for Amy was very different than for other children.

Sharon describes Amy's vision. "She couldn't see colors: She had no depth perception. The only things she could see were three to five inches in front of her nose. When we say she had vision, she really didn't have that much vision. She saw lights and shadows."

She also had a very positive attitude and embraced life, seemingly unaware of her handicap.

"Her development was perfectly normal," says Sharon. "We never treated her any different from anyone else. She was such a happy child."

But as Amy approached school age, it was suggested that she be placed in a facility for the blind.

Sharon resisted this suggestion. "When I was told that she should be enrolled in a blind school, I told the lady there was no way I was ever going to teach my daughter to be blind. That wasn't fair to her; she had her whole future ahead of her. I was going to work as hard as I could to teach her how to be normal, to get along in a normal world. I really believe that anybody can do anything, if they figure out how to do it."

Amy's lack of vision did not translate as a lack of

intelligence or eagerness to learn. And with the help of family, friends, and teachers, she excelled.

Amy remembers, "I didn't let it bother me. I think I was too young to really realize that I was different.

"I basically asked a lot of questions. That was my main way of doing it. But I did have other tools. I used some magnifying glasses and I had paper that had extra big and extra dark lines so that I could tell where the lines were. I wasn't going to let my eyes get in the way. I was pretty stubborn."

Amy's mother agrees, saying, "Amy was a straight-A student, honor roll, all kinds of awards. She'd try anything. She'd do anything. Learning to ask for help was the most difficult thing for Amy to do."

Amy's astonishing progress continued until shortly after entering high school, when she faced a new challenge that no one had expected.

"I'd always had good days and bad days with my sight," Amy says. "Some days it'd be harder for me to see things. They'd be foggier or it seemed like everything was a little bit darker. During October and November of my freshman year, it just seemed like I had a lot more bad days than good days. I'd have to strain my eyes a little bit more. I'd get more headaches. One morning I got up and my vision was gone. I couldn't see anything."

Virtually overnight, Amy had gone completely blind.

Amy returned to her optometrist, Dr. Burkart. Sharon describes the results of his examination. "Dr. Burkart told us that the retina that had been healthy in the past was now starting to disappear, and we said, 'Modern medicine is so amazing nowadays, isn't there anything we can do?' He said no. She was going to be blind the rest of her life."

The doctor couldn't explain this change in Amy's condition. "I don't have an answer as to why this happened. It's not something we would typically expect."

"That was probably the most difficult thing for us to understand," Sharon continues. "We had been told it wouldn't get any worse. We had always been told her vision was always gonna be this way."

But the doctors had been wrong, and after fourteen years of partial sight, Amy was faced with total darkness. Amy was now totally and irreparably blind.

"I used the cane to get around," Amy says. "To me, using the cane kind of labeled me as someone with a handicap. 'Oh, look, she can't see.' It just made me feel not as good as everyone else."

Sharon recalls her daughter's emotions at the time. "She was devastated. There were moments when she cried and cried, you know, 'Why me? Why did this have to happen to me?' But Amy has got this spirit that is incredible. She said, 'Okay, Mom, I think I'm done crying. And we have to go on.'"

And life did go on, only this time Amy turned to her friends with a new sense of appreciation.

She describes her new relationships. "I'd always had to ask for help from my friends. But now I really had to rely on them. I'd spend hours on the phone with friends, having them help me with homework. It was really nice. It was a lot easier on me. I couldn't imagine what I would have done without friends."

While Amy was grateful to her friends, when it came to geometry, Michael McGregor was more than happy to help.

Michael explains, "Amy was really strong in math. She would help me, because I'm nowhere near as strong in math. I would read her the problems or I would draw the shapes for her and she could feel them. She would help me work out all the math problems, because I couldn't do it on my own. So we worked as a team.

"Throughout the whole ordeal, Amy had a great attitude; she just had a wonderful outlook on life. It was just really pleasant to be around her. She was very inspirational."

Amy's rapid adjustment to blindness amazed everyone. She trained to use a seeing-eye dog and learned to read Braille, which can take years, in a matter of months.

"When I lost my sight, I was told that it would not come back. Period. End of story," says Amy. "I always hoped that it would come back, but I never really sat there thinking, Oh, I'm gonna be blind forever, feeling sorry for myself. I never really let myself do that. I tried to keep myself busy and do as much as I could."

Amy's ability to see beyond her limitations found expression in everything she did. "In drill team I felt like I had no problem, because I was out there doing what a bunch of other girls who had perfect sight were doing, and I was completely blind. Dancing was my way to get away. I could do it. I didn't have to worry about not being able to see."

Amy's joy in dance was inspiring to everyone who witnessed it. Her teammate Sarah Potts was especially impressed.

"I was incredibly amazed to watch Amy perform," says Sarah. "When she would get out there, she would be on beat, on cue. Everything was perfect with her when she was performing. It was the most amazing thing to watch."

Sharon applauds her daughter's courage. "She was so well-adjusted, I think she helped all of us be well-adjusted. She didn't let us fall apart. You can't fall apart; you gotta do this. 'Just make sure I match when I walk out the door,' she'd say. That's the way we coped with it."

After more than a year of total blindness, Amy's life was as happy and active as it had ever been. Then in January of 2000, everything changed once again.

"I have a talking program on my computer," Amy says. "I was talking to one of my friends, and all of a sudden I started to note a difference in my vision. I was kind of like, Okay, whatever. And I just kept talking and it was no big deal. Then I started to notice a really big change—I could tell there was stuff on my computer. And that's when I realized I could really see.

"When I first got my sight back, I was excited, but I was scared because I'd never really seen anything. I'd always seen shadows. I'd never seen clear things. And that's what was in the mirror. It was a perfect reflection of me. And I had never experienced anything like that before. I didn't know what blue was or purple or anything. I didn't know what a chair looked like!"

Dr. Burkart was one of the first to receive Amy's incredible news.

He remembers the call. "Amy called me up and said, 'Dr. Burkart, I can see out of my right eye.' I said, 'Okay,

Amy, meet me at the office tomorrow morning first thing and let's take a look at it and see what's going on.' "

At the examination, the results were remarkable when Amy attempted to read the doctor's eye chart.

"I was incredibly amazed at how well she was seeing," says Dr. Burkart. "I could see the smile come on her face when she could see those letters."

Dr. Burkart's amazement wouldn't end there. Within a few days, both of Amy's eyes had cleared.

"The fascinating thing when I examined her," he says, "was that there was nothing different that would lead me to believe she would regain her vision to the level that she did. I could see the coloboma. I could see the swelling on the eye.

"In my mind, there's no explanation why Amy is seeing as well as she is. And she's seeing better now than she did the first time I examined her. In my mind, that's a miracle."

Amy says, "Now I could see out of both eyes, so it was really neat. I didn't have to just try and look out of one eye. We were walking down the street and I thought, Wow, I can read the signs."

Sharon recalls her daughter's joy at her recovery. "She'd never seen the mountains before. She'd never seen the ocean before. She'd never seen any of this. There's a whole new world out there. You want your kids to have everything, and here she was just bouncing around. She was so happy. And then there's a certain amount of you that thinks, Is it gonna last?"

"It could be gone tomorrow," Amy admits. "It could be gone in five minutes. Deep down I'm afraid I might lose it again, but I'm trying to live in the present right now and not really worry about what could happen tomorrow or what could happen next week. Just take advantage of what I have now.

"I don't want to miss something because I'm worrying that maybe I won't see tomorrow. I just want to experience everything I can, while I still can."

"It was a miracle," Sharon concludes. "It was a gift from God. She'd been through an awful lot in fourteen, fifteen years. And she deserved to get her sight back. There's an old saying: Stop and smell the roses. When you have someone who's visually impaired, you have to stop and smell the roses and you have to stop and feel the roses. Amy's really taught us how to see. Not only with our eyes, but with our hearts."

# EXTRAORDINARY RESCUES

Amy Maxwell was sixteen years old and living with her family in Huntsville, Alabama, when she became involved with a fellow high school student named David.

As Amy explains, "We didn't date for very long, and I got pregnant. I was seventeen and living at home, so halfway through my pregnancy, he started to live with us at my dad's house. After Bradley was born, he lived there for about two or three months and then we split up."

Young Bradley became the center of a bitter custody fight between his teenaged parents. When he was two, they both hired lawyers, and a custody hearing was set for January 1999.

"A week before Christmas he called me, real upset," Amy remembers, "and was crying and wanted to see Bradley for Christmas. So I told him that he could get him that Tuesday morning, but he had to have him home Christmas Eve, because we had family coming." David agreed, and arrived at Amy's house on schedule to pick Bradley up.

"He picked him up Tuesday morning and Christmas Eve comes," continues Amy, "and he doesn't show up. So I start thinking, Well, maybe I'm supposed to go get him. So I go to his house and nobody answers the door. I went around to the back door and he's in there talking, but he won't answer the door. The glass is missing from one of the panes on the door, so I reached in and opened the door."

Amy went inside to find her son, but what she discovered caught her completely off guard. David accused Amy of breaking and entering, and held her at gunpoint.

Says Amy, "He had a shotgun pointed at me, and had 911 on the phone and told 911 that somebody was breaking into the house and he was going to shoot them. He wouldn't say where Bradley was. And since, legally, neither one of us had custody, he was with anyone who physically had him."

A week later, the day before the custody hearing, David had still not returned her son . . . and the situation was about to explode. Early that morning, after Amy's boyfriend left for work, David approached the house.

"I got up at about 7:30," Amy remembers. "I let the dog out to go to the bathroom, and I left the door kind of cracked, because that's what I usually do. I went back into my room to get my clothes out of the closet."

Moments later, David entered the house through the open door and quietly climbed the stairs to Amy's bedroom.

She describes the situation. "I'm standing at the closet and I saw something out of the corner of my eye as I turned. He grabbed me and we fell back into my closet. He had a roll of tape in his hand, and he was trying to get my arms together to tape them. We fought for about twenty minutes before he actually was physically able to sit on me and get my arms taped together, and then he taped me at my knees and my wrists and my ankles."

David demanded the keys to Amy's car. When she told him she didn't know where they were, he stormed off in search of them himself.

"He went outside to get the car keys," says Amy, "and I was trying to find the cordless phone. When I found it, I tried to dial 911."

But before she could dial the numbers, David was back in the room.

"He tried to suffocate me. He covered my mouth and covered my nose. I struggled with him and then I pretended to pass out," Amy recalls.

As she lay there, pretending to be unconscious, David wrapped her limp body in a blanket and carried her out the back door. Amy describes the terrifying scene that met her there. "I see my car with the trunk open, and I thought, Oh my God, I'm going in the trunk. He put me in the trunk, shut the trunk, got in the car, and drove."

Where was David taking her? What would he do when

they got there? Amy wasted no time working the tape off her face and then started on her hands.

"He had taped my hands in front of me," she explains. "So all I had to really do was just get it with my teeth and unroll it, and once I had my hands undone, I just took it off my legs.

"I mean, I rode in there forever. The whole time, I'm going between crying and praying and freaking out, and the next thing I remember was that I heard on the radio that it was set to Chattanooga USO; that's their radio station. I was like, I'm in Tennessee. Nobody knows that I'm gone from my house. Nobody's going to know I'm gone."

After several hours on the road, David was forced to stop for gas. Amy had no idea where or why he'd stopped until she heard the gas cap coming off. It was then that she began kicking and screaming for help. David just turned the radio up as loud as it would go, so that no one would hear Amy's cries. But he'd underestimated her ingenuity in the face of danger.

Amy remembered that "the speaker wires run in the back of the trunk, so I ripped the speaker wires and started screaming and kicking the trunk. I could hear him run around the car and jump back in. And he took off."

It was a great idea, yet it failed to attract the attention of anyone who could help. But it helped to convince Amy that she wasn't powerless.

"That's where I got the idea to take out the brake lights," Amy continues. "I took all the taillights out, because they just kind of snap in. I was thinking maybe he would get pulled over for not having any brake lights or taillights. And then I thought that that's gonna require a police officer to get behind us and to actually see, and then pull him over. So then I started thinking about stuff that was in my car.

"My car has a standard jack that comes with it, and the handle comes off. I shoved it through the hole and busted out the taillight and I could see that we were on the highway; I could see behind me. Whenever cars would get close, I would start sticking stuff out of the taillight, like paper towels, and my finger, the jack handle, and the light—I would stick the light in the hole and try to flash."

None of the passing motorists seemed to take any notice of her desperate attempts to get their attention. But Amy was about to experience a miracle. Four hours after Amy's ordeal began, another couple, Teri and Dale Schroeder, experienced an unusual set of delays as they returned from their vacation. They'd started out later than planned, stopping at an unscheduled place on the map, and left just in time to end up behind Amy's car. As they followed the car, something caught Dale's eye.

Dale explains, "The taillight lens was broken, but the light bulb disappeared out of the hole and then it came back in the hole. I said to Teri, 'There's something strange about the back of that car. Watch that. Let's see what happens with it.'"

Amy says, "I had thought at one time that a car was following us, but then they would back off. I thought that nobody knew I was there."

But Dale Schroeder wasn't giving up yet. "I said, 'Well, I'm gonna just watch it for a while,' so I caught back up with him and stayed behind him. And pretty soon, paper started coming out of this little hole in the taillight and then a tire tool would come out, wiggle around, and then go back in. At one time, Teri said that she thought she saw a finger, and we thought maybe it was a college prank. We pulled up beside the car and passed him, and Teri said, 'No, there's nothing out of the ordinary on the inside.' "

Teri continues the dramatic story. "There had to be someone locked in the trunk. It couldn't be anything else. Basically, every scenario we could come up with was not good, so we decided we'd better do something."

The couple debated calling the police, but Teri was afraid the cops would "think we're loons." Eventually, however, they decided to take the chance.

"It's just not something you see every day," says Teri, "so you just don't consider that somebody's actually locked in the trunk. But we thought, Well, if we're stupid, we're stupid, but if not . . ."

A little embarrassed, and unsure of what was happening, Dale and Teri felt they couldn't let it go, so they called 911.

Teri says, "We told them, 'We don't know if it's really something, but we think it's strange.' And they took it seriously right away."

Dale and Teri stayed on the phone with the emergency operator. Dale describes their experience. "They would ask us what location we were at, what exit, what mile marker, and we'd tell them. And then I finally told them, 'Well, we just passed a police car back there,' and they came back and said, 'Okay, he's got you in sight.' "

Meanwhile, Amy was still hoping that her plan had worked. "I didn't even know that someone had called 911," she remembers. "I didn't even know that anybody had told the police. I didn't have any idea. When I saw the police car, I started putting the light in there and sticking stuff out, fast. And they pulled him over. And when they pulled us over, I started just screaming and hitting the trunk."

The Tennessee State troopers pulled David over and got him out of the car. One of them unlocked the trunk and freed Amy Maxwell. Amy was taken to the hospital and released without injury. David was taken to jail, where he remains today.

Amy still thinks about her terrible ordeal. "I was okay. I was just a little scratched, a little bruised, really scared. He never said, really, what he was planning on doing. And I really don't like to speculate because it's just scary."

During his interrogation, David told authorities that their son was safe in his grandfather's care.

"The first time I saw my son in two weeks was four o'clock in the morning—and I woke him up. The next morning, I got up and went to court.

"The judge awarded me full custody, and any visitation with his family is at my discretion," says Amy.

Several weeks later, Amy was finally able to meet the Schroeders and thank them for what they had done. They formed an instant bond.

Amy says, "They're like family now. They're people that I intend to be in touch with forever."

And Teri agrees. "We have a connection. Now it will

be a lifelong connection—as far as we're concerned, she's one of our children now. She's kind of been adopted into our family."

Today, Amy's happily raising her son, thanks to the Schroeders and the miraculous set of circumstances that put their lives together. As Teri points out, "We left at noon rather than at six in the morning like we always did. We stopped early, which was unusual, and then the next morning we started late, which put us on an intercept course with that car, which I believe was God's timing."

Amy feels the same way, saying, "Truly, I believe that somewhere, some divine power put me in touch with the Schroeders, to find me and get me home to my son. That would be the miracle, I think."

# CAPTAIN TO THE RESCUE

It was late at night in the winter of 1981 when Fire Captain Ed Cushing suddenly awoke from a terrifying dream. The details were so clear that even twenty years later, he still remembers them as if they'd happened yesterday.

"I jumped up around four in the morning, and I was full of sweat," he says. "I had just had the strangest dream. There was a fire and I saved three people. It was in an older neighborhood. And people were yelling that there were three people in the house. They told me that there were two children and a mother."

In his dream, Ed suddenly found himself inside the inferno, searching for the victims.

"It was very dense smoke," he recalls. "You couldn't see your hand in front of you, so I was just feeling my way. And I felt the body, and it was the mother."

He rushed the unconscious woman outside, where he began administering CPR in a desperate attempt to save her life.

Ed continues, "I ran back inside the house to find the children. Sure enough, I come across one of the kids and I get him out. But I know there's a third one. But the smoke is so thick now that I'm crawling up the stairs, and sure enough . . . in the hallway outside the bedroom I find the other boy. Then I get outside and the chief is standing there, and he says to me, 'Good job, Cushing.' That was my dream. I saved three people all by myself.

"When I was raised, my mother always counted on dreams. As a warning, or a sign that something's gonna happen."

A few hours later, after Ed reported to duty, an alarm came in for a major house fire.

Ed remembers the call. "It was only five blocks from the firehouse, so we got there within a minute and a half. The first four people told me that they had made it out the back door. But there were people in the house on the second floor."

No one knew for sure how many victims were still trapped inside. Ed rushed into the building.

"When I got to the second floor," says Ed, "the door was locked. So I had to kick it in. The mother was right outside her door and when I started to pick her up to carry her outside, I saw a leg, and then I knew there was somebody else, so I had to come back.

"I took her down, and I laid her on the grass. Her heart wasn't beating for quite a while, maybe four minutes. And it's supposed to be three minutes, you're dead. And so I said, 'Please, God.' Next time I gave a compression, her heart just beat."

While another fireman administered oxygen, Ed raced back into the house.

"I got the boy. And I put my hand over to grab him. He said, 'Mommy?' and I said, 'No, this is the fireman. You're all right now.' So I just put him on the ground next to the lady. All he needed was the fresh air."

It was at that moment that Ed realized what was happening.

He says, "It dawned on me that I was reliving the dream."

And if the dream was accurate, it meant that there was a third person still trapped inside the raging fire.

By now, huge flames and thick smoke enveloped the building, but Ed knew exactly where he was going.

"The dream led me through the fire," Ed explains. "Everything in that dream was true of the actual fire."

He remembered that the boy was at the top of the stairs.

"I made it, crawling up the stairs on my belly. And I actually went to where he was, as if I knew where he was."

The child wasn't breathing, and Ed couldn't find a pulse or a heartbeat.

"He was small," recalls Ed, "and I could give him CPR by just pushing on his chest and blowing into his face on the way down, and his heart just started up again. And when I got that, I went out and I said, 'Thank you, God.' I had goose pimples all over me. I just said thank you."

And then, just as in his dream, the fire chief approached Ed.

"Good job, Cushing, but I don't think the mother and the little boy are going to make it," the chief said.

Ed replied, "Oh, no, Chief, they're going to make it."

"How do you know?" asked the chief.

"Because I had this dream last night," Ed answered. "I saw the whole thing. Now, believe me, Chief, they're gonna make it."

And Ed now says, "I had no doubt in my mind of this. You know, I got the message from upstairs."

Several hours later, the final chapter in Ed's dream became a reality when the woman he rescued, Suzette Tomaselli, regained consciousness.

Suzette remembers, "I didn't even know I was alive yet, really. I woke up and I saw my sister, and I said, 'Oh, my God, where are the boys?' "

Her son, Michael, was recovering in another room.

"I remember finally coming to in a hospital and being in this oxygen tent," says Michael. "And looking over, I saw my cousin, and wondered what happened."

Michael's cousin, Martin, continues, "The next thing I remember is waking up in the hospital, and the light was on, and my eyes were really sensitive. I said, 'Turn the light out, it's hurting my eyes.' "

The miracle was complete.

But it wasn't until Captain Cushing visited the family in the hospital that they learned how truly miraculous their rescue had been.

Ed told Suzette that he had dreamed of the fire the night before it happened.

Suzette recalls, "He said, 'I had a premonition about this whole fire. I knew that there were going to be three people in this fire and they were almost going to die, but they were going to live to make it.' He even told me the layout of our apartment. He started saying all these things about Martin being at the top of the stairs. That he knew he was there."

"He told me about the premonition," Martin says, "and I was just amazed. He knew right where to go and get me. I guess that was God's way of saying, 'This is your second chance.' "

For Suzette, that second chance at life would mean a second marriage. And Captain Cushing was there to give the bride away.

"I asked Captain Cushing, 'Would you give me away at my wedding? I mean, I'm here because you gave me my life back.' He kind of grinned and said he'd be glad to," says Suzette.

Michael remembers the event fondly. "Captain Cushing giving my mom away really touched all the family. You know what I mean? It was so appropriate."

Today, Suzette, Martin, and Michael still feel a sense of deep gratitude to the man who saved their lives, as well as a profound sense of wonder at the circumstances that guided him.

For who can explain how a man waking from a dream can find himself in the same exact situation a few hours later?

Or how that dream could lead him back into the blazing building to find a child that otherwise would have surely died?

There is, perhaps, only one explanation.

"I really believe in miracles, and I believe that there's somebody watching," says Suzette.

Michael agrees. "The way he did everything was perfect. He knew just what to do."

"If he didn't have that dream," Martin wonders, "where would I be today? I wouldn't even be here. Words can't express our gratitude to him."

# BUMPER RIDE HORROR

The morning of March 30, 1999, started out like any other for the Tafoya household. Judy and Lincoln Tafoya and their nanny, Angel Garcia, were getting six young children off to school.

Judy says, "We had just gotten back from Arizona from a business trip, so we got up in the morning and Angel was getting them all dressed and fed and ready to go."

Judy was transmitting new credit-card orders for the family pottery business, while Lincoln and Angel herded everyone out the door.

"I take them to school, or sometimes to the bus stop," says Lincoln. "But this time I was running late, so I had to take them all the way to school. And I said, 'Well, everybody load up.' "

In the confusion that followed, only Angel noticed three-year-old Chelsea heading out the front door behind the other children.

Angel recalls, "I said, 'Where are you going?' and she said, 'I'm going with my dad. He's going to take me to school,' and I said, " 'Okay, honey.' "

Outside, as Lincoln climbed into his truck and started the engine, Chelsea ran to catch up. When she couldn't, the little girl made a terrible mistake.

As Lincoln sped off, a neighbor spotted Chelsea on the back bumper. He took off after Lincoln on foot, but the car was going too fast.

Judy was still entering numbers on the credit-card machine when her neighbor raced to the door. Says Judy, "He told me, 'Did you know that one of the babies is hanging on the back of the car?' "

Angel remembers, "I heard her say, 'Oh, yeah, she probably rode with her dad. The kids are all going to school,' and he goes, 'No, you don't understand—not in the car, outside the car.' "

The neighbor returned to his own home and Judy shouted for Angel. "My stomach went up into my throat," says Judy, "and I was yelling and telling her, 'Get on the phone and call 911, or somebody!' "

Judy rushed outside to their other car to chase after Lincoln, while Angel went to the phone . . . but there was a problem.

"I went to go use the phone, and the phone line was dead," explains Angel.

What she didn't know was that the phone line was tied up by the credit-card machine and could not dial out.

Outside, Judy tried to start the car, but the engine refused to turn over.

Angel says, "I didn't know what to do and I was going crazy. I didn't know how to tell Judy that I couldn't get through, because I didn't know what was going on."

Meanwhile, Lincoln was racing toward school, trying to beat the clock, unaware of his baby daughter clinging to the rear bumper for her life. It was at that moment that Connie Romero first spotted Chelsea. She was driving to work and pulled onto the road behind the Tafoyas' truck.

Says Connie, "I just saw this image in the back, on the bumper. And something just kept drawing my attention to that image. I kept thinking to myself, Well, it's probably a spare. And then as I got closer, I could see that it was a little figure.

"My first thought was, Geez, who would play such a cruel joke on somebody, because April Fool's Day was the next day."

But as she sped up to get a closer look, Connie realized that what she was seeing was not a joke.

"As I started to gain on the traffic again," she describes, "I looked at that image and it looked so real . . . and as I saw the hair blowing, that's when I realized that it was a child on the back bumper."

Her adrenaline pumping, Connie began urgently flashing her lights and honking her horn to get the driver's attention.

Lincoln remembers, "I noticed this lady behind me, and she kind of freaked me out a little bit. You see a lot of road rage when you travel a lot."

Lincoln veered around a horseshoe curve, hoping to lose the driver behind him.

He continues, "I looked back there to see if that lady's still coming up. And I noticed that she was coming up pretty fast, so I thought, Oh, what's going on here? What did I do? Did I do something wrong?"

In the meantime, says Connie, "I got even closer to the vehicle. That's when she turned around and looked at me. The first thought that went through my mind was, this is a little kid that's gonna fall off the bumper.

"If I get too close and she should fall off, she's gonna come through my windshield. If she falls off and she rolls, I'm gonna run right over her."

Connie kept honking her horn and continued to cross into the other lane, putting her own life in jeopardy to flag Lincoln down. Luckily, her cell phone was in the car, and she managed to contact the local police and alert them to the desperate situation.

Meanwhile, Judy Tafoya tried desperately to start her car, but the engine refused to turn over. With every passing minute, the chances of saving her daughter grew slimmer and slimmer.

Judy says, "I ran back in and I said, 'I'm going to see if I can get one of the neighbors to run after them.' I ran to three houses and knocked on the doors, and nobody answered. Then I ran back down and I kicked over the Suburban till it finally started."

With terrifying images racing through her mind, Judy frantically scanned the sides of the road for Chelsea.

"I was saying, Lord, if I have any chips up there, I'm cashing them in," Judy recalls. "I specifically told Him that I didn't even want a hair on her head hurt, but my mind was telling me to be logical, that's a really heavy-traffic road."

Back on Los Alamos Highway, at speeds up to 70 miles per hour, Connie was still trying desperately to get Lincoln to pull over.

"My adrenaline was just going so high," she says, "that the only thing I could think of was to get the attention of the driver."

In a bold effort to put an end to this highly dangerous situation, Connie pulled a daredevil stunt.

She describes the scene. "He was getting ready to pass a vehicle and I sped up and stayed even with him so that he didn't have the opportunity to get in the passing lane. He finally looked at me, and when he did, I made the sign for him to pull over."

Lincoln remembers, "She pulled up in front of me and she jumped out and said, 'There's a kid behind your car.' And I look at her, you know, Yeah, right. We looked in the back of the vehicle, but there was no kid."

"I was shaking so bad," says Connie. "I just couldn't figure out where we had lost her, because I had followed him for so many miles."

Suddenly, little Chelsea appeared from around the front of the truck.

Connie says, "Her dad looked at her, and the expression on his face was just . . . he was in total shock."

Lincoln agrees. "When I realized I could have lost her, my heart was just ready to pop."

Moments later, Judy spotted the cars on the side of the road. "I felt Chelsea's little body; she had been on that car for quite a while. The cold was inside her bones. But she had not a scrape on her. Not a hair was moved, and I just thanked the Lord."

Later, Judy asked Chelsea what was going through her mind when she climbed on the back of her dad's truck that morning.

"My daddy was taking the kids to school and I wanted to go," Chelsea answers.

For everyone, Chelsea's survival was nothing short of a miracle.

Lincoln insists, "It had to be a miracle for a little kid like that to hang on going that fast and hitting that many bumps. Had to be a miracle."

And to the Tafoyas, Connie Romero will always be a part of that miracle.

Says Lincoln, "Connie Romero, she's a godsend. I don't think anybody else would have stuck with us."

"Right past where they stopped," adds Judy, "there are about three dips in the road that are really, really bad. I know if they had hit them, that Chelsea wouldn't have hung on."

Connie concludes, "Being a mother myself, I can't even imagine what Judy went through that morning. It was a really good feeling to know that I had saved the life of a child."

# Mini Driver

It started out like any other Saturday morning, as retired farmer Benny Hester headed out to do his daily chores. And as anyone in Gadsden, Alabama, will tell you, wherever Benny goes, his eight-year-old grandson, Dean, is sure to follow.

Says Dean, "He always does stuff with me. He always drives the truck with me, and I feed the cows and horses and everything."

Even Helen Hester is astonished by the bond between her husband and grandson.

"Dean and his PawPaw are extremely close. They do everything together," Helen says. "They mow grass; they plow the garden. They drive trucks, tractors. They have fun. Dean has been with us most of his life. His PawPaw kept him when his mother went back to work after he was born. And then gradually, he just got to where he stayed with us all the time."

On this particular day, Benny and Dean were keeping a promise to feed a neighbor's cows while he was away. Their first stop: to pick up a load of hay at the barn. Normally a man full of boundless energy, today Benny felt oddly fatigued and short of breath. But a promise was a promise.

Dean remembers, "I just wanted to tell him to take it easy. He was getting too hot."

And so, moving more slowly than usual, he finished loading the truck. As they began driving across the open field to where the cows were grazing, Benny continued to feel ill, but he pressed on toward the pasture.

The creek was higher than usual, but they were already so far from the main road that Benny decided to chance crossing it. Halfway across, he realized how lucky they were not to have gotten stuck. Fifteen minutes later, they arrived at the pasture and began unloading the hay.

As Dean recalls, "We were feeding the cows and he was cutting the bales and just raking it off in a circle and he just hollered, 'Ho!' and I stopped. He leaned over the back of the truck and he rested and he said, 'Go on.' When we got done, he fell down on the ground. I got him up. I don't know how I managed to get him up."

Even eight-year-old Dean knew that something was terribly wrong, and that they were too far away to run for help. So he climbed behind the driver's seat of the one-ton pickup, and turned the key.

"I knew I had to do it, because no one could have found us where we were. We were way back there. It was scary because I knew he was sick, because he was laying down like that," says Dean.

Barely able to reach the pedals, the small boy continued driving. As he drove across the field, there was only one thing on little Dean's mind.

He says, "The thought of losing my PawPaw was bad, very bad, because we had always done stuff together."

Benny needed immediate medical attention. But the quickest route to the main road meant going back the way they'd come, which also meant recrossing the creek. To get stuck now would be disastrous. And the eight-year-old boy hesitated.

"I reached down and grabbed another gear and I got it in first and floored it through the creek," remembers Dean.

When they finally reached the main road, Dean stopped, hoping to flag down a passing driver. But the road was deserted. It was then that Dean remembered the cell phone his grandfather kept inside the truck's glove compartment, and called his grandmother.

Helen remembers, "When he said Benny was laying in the seat and couldn't drive, that scared me. Benny's not a complainer. He never complains. I knew if it was a virus or a headache or something like that, he wouldn't be laying in the seat. I knew it had to be something serious. So I went up there to see about him, and when I got there, he was slumped over in the seat. It was extremely frightening. It was horrible—I thought that was going to be it. I thought it was it. He was quiet as a piece of cotton. But I didn't know if he was alive or dead when I first got there, because he was just slumped over in his seat and wouldn't answer me.

"He's been the force that's kept this family all together, has kept us moving and going the right way. So I didn't know what would happen to us if we didn't have him."

Moments later, paramedics arrived on the scene.

"I was so worried about Benny that Dean slipped my mind for a few minutes," says Helen. "I started looking for him and he was standing over by the fence crying. It finally had gotten to him that his PawPaw was really sick. I told him that the ambulance was there and they were gonna take care of him."

Benny was taken to nearby Riverview Regional Medical Center, where he was rushed into surgery. Meanwhile, Helen and Dean anxiously waited, not knowing what had gone wrong. After hours of wondering whether Benny would live or die, Dr. Peter Szeto arrived with the answer.

Dr. Szeto explains, "Mr. Hester was having a heart attack. One of his coronary arteries, the one that supplies blood to the bottom part of the heart—what we call the right coronary artery—was completely blocked."

Dr. Szeto told Helen and Dean, "I have good news for you. He is doing fine. He had a blocked artery; we opened it up. It's very stable now."

Benny's life had been saved thanks to the quick thinking of his eight-year-old grandson.

"If he didn't come, you know, within the next ten minutes, he might have died," says Dr. Szeto.

As Benny put it, "I owe a lot to my grandson. He actually saved my life, because if I had been by myself over in that field with nobody around for miles, I would have surely died."

Helen agrees. "It was a miracle because I have my husband now, and I don't believe I would've had him otherwise. And it's a miracle because the good Lord gave us Dean to be with him at that particular time, or we wouldn't have him."

Each new day is a precious gift to Benny, who treasures every moment he spends watching his grandson grow up.

"Me and Dean have a great relationship," says Benny. "He is the apple of my eye, if you want to know the truth about it. I guess I love him more than anything in the world."

# COMPASSIONATE CREATURES

# PATRA'S GIFT

In 1998, Donna Jacobs and her husband, John, were leading full, active lives, with some very adventurous plans.

"We love to travel," Donna says. "Our goal was to
travel through all fifty states on a motorcycle before we're
fifty."

But their plans were about to change.

"John and I had taken a motorcycle trip to Alaska on
the Al–Can Highway. From the beginning of this trip, I was
extremely tired. I was having problems with balance. Upon
coming home, I noticed that I was having excruciating migraines."

The intense headaches soon left her virtually home-
bound.

John says, "It was kind of surprising. We were living such an active life before. Now we're kind of slowing down. Donna's having trouble. But it's quite a change of lifestyle. For several days, Donna was having bad migraines. I came back from the store, where I'd been grocery shopping."

Donna had felt well enough to help out that day, but she was about to suffer a massive, agonizing pain in her head.

"It was quite scary for me to see her lying there. She was conscious but she wasn't talking very clearly, and her mouth was drawn to one side. The doctor at the hospital asked her to describe the pain, and she told him it was sharp."

The next day, a physical examination determined that Donna had suffered from a transischemic attack.

Donna says, "A transischemic attack is when small blood vessels burst in the brain. And that was what was happening to me."

"They kept running tests on her," John remembers. "They couldn't find anything that was causing the problems."

Donna says, "I lost confidence with my doctors. I wanted my life back, and I was getting worse. Six months later I began having seizures. That was very frightening. I've always felt like I was in control of my life, and now there was something else that was controlling me."

John was worried. "I was getting more concerned because as time went on, she was showing more depression. She didn't want anyone to see her anymore. She was afraid she was going to have a seizure out in public. The seizure itself wasn't so bad, it was the thought of having one: not knowing it was coming, where she would be when it came, who would be around her."

"I turned off the telephone, closed the curtains, and stayed in my home," Donna says.

John watched helplessly as his wife withdrew from the world.

"I was very concerned about her. But this was something that was out of my control. I had no way to help her. There was nothing I could do about it. The doctors couldn't help her, and I couldn't help her. One day I told her that she had to get back into life a little bit, and she answered, 'I don't have a life.'"

And then, a casual offer from a friend provided a ray of hope.

"A friend of mine had some puppies she wanted to give away," John remembers, "and I thought this might help bring her out of depression."

Donna says, "And I didn't know if I wanted a puppy. John said, 'Well, someone is giving these puppies away, they need homes. Let's go get one.' So we did. And there was one female and two males. I knew I wanted a female, so I picked her up. And John says, 'Wait a minute, look at that one down here.'"

John says, "There was something about one of the male pups that just caught my eye. He was staring at me. He made good eye contact. And the expressions on his face! I said, 'Donna, this is the puppy we need, right here. I don't care if it's a male. I think this is the one we should take.'"

Donna says, "I knew how excited John was. I said, 'Okay, if you want a puppy, fine. That puppy will be your puppy. I have my puppy.'"

Caring for the puppies gave Donna a new purpose in life.

"They needed my attention," she says. "I found myself getting out of bed and playing with them. And they were a joy."

Donna named the dogs Cleo and Patra, two halves of a whole: Cleopatra. But tragedy was about to strike. Cleo was diagnosed with a fatal parasitic disease.

Donna says, "Four months later, we lost her. She died. And when she died, I began to be depressed again, because I was losing something else. She was my favorite."

Shortly after Cleo's death, Patra began exhibiting some very strange behavior.

Donna remembers, "He began knocking me down and keeping me down, and I had to worry about my physical well-being."

The attacks would soon become more frequent and more violent. The pair of puppies had brought her back to life, but when Patra began attacking her without warning, Donna's veterinarian suggested she contact a canine behavior specialist.

Donna says, "And I thought, A canine behavior specialist? I've never heard of that. What does she do?"

Her curiosity led her to a meeting with Kathy Cramer.

Kathy says, "Donna had bruises on her arms and legs caused by Patra. It was horrible."

Donna says, "She asked me if the puppy did this to me.

And I said, 'Yes, this puppy hates me. He doesn't listen to me, and I can't get him to do the sits and downs, which he does beautifully for John. He just doesn't like me.' "

Kathy says, "So I asked him to do some basic commands, and he did them perfectly for me."

Kathy left Donna with some training exercises to practice with Patra.

Kathy says, "I came back in two weeks and the behavior was still the same. And I thought, This dog is trying to communicate something to this woman. I asked her, 'Donna, I don't want to pry into your personal life at all, but do you have any neurological problems?' "

"I began to cry," Donna recalls, "because I thought it was visible. And I thought I was doing so much better that no one could tell."

"I told her, 'Actually, your dog is telling you there is something wrong,' " Kathy remembers. "I told her that when he licked her hands like he'd been doing, she should lie down on the ground on her back and see what happens. We're beginning to believe that people with seizures emit an odor that we cannot sense, but dogs, with their great senses of smell, can."

And what Donna had believed to be attacks were actually Patra's way of telling her that something was wrong... of alerting her to the fact that she was about to have a seizure.

Kathy says, "I don't think that the seizure-alerting is a common ability in every dog. I told her that I thought Patra would make an excellent seizure-alert dog for her."

This would not happen without hard work. Kathy

spent the next six months training Donna and Patra to understand and trust each other.

"We modified his behavior," Kathy says. "Instead of pulling on her clothes like he was, we modified it until he would just lick her hands."

Donna says, "When Patra starts nudging my hand and licking my fingers, I know that I have very little time to lie down. What he wanted, with all this misbehaving, was to let me know that something was wrong, that I had to stop what I was doing and lie down, and he knew what to do."

Kathy says, "Donna even told me that one time she was lying down and she felt perfectly fine, had felt the seizure had passed, but that Patra kept pushing her back down. And in about ten minutes, she had another one."

Patra had given Donna a new sense of security. But was it enough to allow her to fully reclaim her life and risk going out in public?

"Kathy asked me, 'How would you like to get back out into life? How would you like to go to a movie again? How would you like to go grocery shopping again? How would you and John like to go out to a nice restaurant and enjoy yourselves?' And I thought, Oh, I don't know about that."

But with Kathy's encouragement, she agreed to give it a try. It had been years since Donna had left her home, and even the simple act of shopping was something foreign and frightening to her.

"She was a little hesitant," Kathy says, "but she was willing to do it. And that is the most courageous thing that a person with a disability can do: take a step outside that disability."

"And that's when my life changed," Donna says. "Kathy told me that we'd passed, that Patra is now a certified service dog. It's a miracle. I have been blessed. Through Patra, I have my life back."

John says, "It was all pretty amazing to me, that this little pup that I had brought home had this ability to alert Donna to a seizure. It definitely made a difference in our lives. Bringing Donna out of her depression and into the life she's leading right now, it's been a miracle."

Donna says, "I never in my wildest dreams would imagine that my guardian angel would come with four paws. And no tail."

# ULU ACTS LIKE LASSIE

During the 1980s, the potbellied pig became a new addition to the list of American household pets. People loved their little piggies, but as they grew to full size and beyond, some owners looked for a way out.

That's how Lulu arrived in the home of Jack and Jo Ann Altsman. Lulu was originally purchased as a present for their daughter Jackie's fortieth birthday, but several weeks later, when Jackie was called out of town, she asked her parents to look after her pig.

"Well, that was a year ago August," remarks Jo Ann, "and we're still baby-sitting Lulu."

During that time, Lulu did what came naturally—she

grew bigger—and she also grew into the hearts and lives of the Altsman family.

"You get attached to them and they get attached to you," says Jack. "They won't leave you. They just want to be where you're at."

"She follows me around a lot," agrees Jo Ann. "I know people who have a dog or a cat under their feet, but I have a 150-pound potbellied pig."

Even their dog, Bear, has come to accept Lulu as a part of the family. When it comes time to take a little vacation, all four of them pile into the truck and head to their mobile home near Lake Erie, where Jack enjoys the fishing and Jo Ann spends the days at the beach with her pig on a blanket.

But on August 4, 1998, their idyllic routine was about to be destroyed.

"My husband got up at five o'clock and went fishing," recalls Jo Ann, "and left Lulu and me and Bear here to go to the beach. When I woke up, it was about a quarter to eight."

As Jo Ann went into the kitchen to start breakfast, she was hit with a strange sensation.

"I was very light-headed and very dizzy," she says, and the next thing she knew, she was on the floor writhing in pain. Jo Ann was having a major heart attack, and the nearest telephone was hundreds of yards away at the trailer park office.

"I kept hollering for help," she says "and no one was coming, so I finally broke a window with an alarm clock."

And still no one responded—except her dog, who

began barking uncontrollably from the bedroom. Perhaps Bear would come to her rescue.

"Our dog is bred to save people in the snow," Jo Ann explains. "He's American Eskimo. He's bred to be a savior."

But the only thing Bear was saving was his strength. He never left the bed and his barking did nothing to summon help.

"I had to face facts," she says. "I was probably going to die."

But before she did, Jo Ann was in for one more surprise: Lulu, standing over her.

"All I could see was her head over my face, which is quite a sight," Jo Ann recalls. Then, as quickly as she appeared, Lulu disappeared. "I could hear her kind of trundling off, but I was very concerned with myself at the time. I had no idea what she was doing."

What Lulu was doing, as it turns out, was leaving the trailer by squeezing through a doggie door, crossing the front yard, and lying down in the road, hoping to stop traffic.

"But nobody would stop," says Jo Ann. "They had no idea what she was. They were afraid of her."

With each rejection, Lulu would return to the house to check on Jo Ann, and then she'd run off for help again. Every time she'd go through the small doggie door, however, her belly would scrape, and by now she was bleeding. But that didn't stop her. Lulu was determined to flag somebody down.

Meanwhile, Jo Ann's condition was worsening.

"So about then, I gave it to God," she says, "and asked God to take care of my husband, because I knew I was really bad."

But Lulu wasn't giving up. She continued to travel between the trailer and the street, hoping that somebody would stop and reward her for performing her favorite trick—"Dead Piggy."

"She knows that if she plays 'Dead Piggy' where we live, the mailman feeds her, the schoolkids feed her like she's starving to death. She knows it works," says Jo Ann.

The sight of a lifeless, bleeding 150-pound pig lying in the middle of the road finally got a passing motorist to stop. And suddenly "Dead Piggy" came to life.

"He followed Lulu back to our trailer, and pounded on the door, saying, 'Hey? Your pig's in distress out here,'" recalls Jo Ann. "And I said to him, 'Oh, thank you, God. Please, I'm really in distress, call 911 for me.'"

The Good Samaritan ran to the park office pay phone to call for help. Minutes later, a team of paramedics arrived on the scene. They stabilized Jo Ann's condition and loaded her into an ambulance to transport her to a local hospital, while Lulu continued to monitor the situation, even attempting to climb into the ambulance with her.

"She just did everything in her power to get in the ambulance. She was going with me and that was it," recalls Jo Ann. "And she's pretty pushy."

Today, Jo Ann has fully recovered from her ordeal, and Lulu has reaped the rewards of being a hero, becoming something of a local celebrity.

"It's unbelievable how the neighbors treat Lulu," remarks Jack. "They come by, and they feed her everything. If she's out in the yard when they get up in the morning, they give her a treat to start her off. The neighbors on the next block, when they come down by us, bring stuff to her."

"They think it's wonderful what the pig did, but they can't believe it," says Jack. "Neither can we, so it had to be a miracle."

Without Lulu by her side, watching over her and tirelessly rushing from the house out into the street to stop traffic, Jo Ann could easily have died that day.

"The heart surgeon told me that fifteen minutes more and I would have had no quality of life, or I would have died," reveals Jo Ann.

But Lulu came to the rescue.

"God sent us Lulu, as funny as that may sound," she says. "Our little angel in her piggy outfit. It was a miracle that Lulu saved my life."

# Dog Rescues Cats

Philip Gonzalez of Long Island, New York, was a guy who had it all. He lived the carefree life of a bachelor and supported it with a good job as a pipe fitter. Then, in 1990, Philip's world came crashing down when he severely injured his arm at a construction site. Doctors told Philip he would never be able to use his arm again.

Philip recalls what the doctors told him. "They told me that the arm was going to wilt away because all the blood vessels and nerves were damaged in there. It would never move again. It would just wilt away, and eventually they would have to amputate. I told them no. I was mad at the world and I wondered, Why me?"

Philip's friend Sheilah Harris tried to pull him out of his depression.

"He was a little bull that was totally incapacitated," says Sheilah, "and that's when I decided that it was just mandatory that we give him a reason to get out of the house, and to me it was as silly as getting a dog."

After initial resistance, Philip accepted his friend Sheilah's suggestion to get a pet. He wound up at a nearby animal shelter. There, Philip met Ginny—immediately, the two made a connection.

Philip describes their first meeting. "She was sitting there looking up at me, smiling, and from that moment on she just hypnotized me. I said, 'You're my dog now. I'm taking you home.' For some reason, we bonded right then and there and she understood that I was injured—that I was gonna take care of her and that she was gonna take care of me."

A few nights later, Ginny began barking for no apparent reason.

"I told her, 'Ginny, be quiet! What are you barking for?'" Philip recalls. "And my hand began to move . . . my right hand, which was never supposed to move; it started to move."

Philip was experiencing a miraculous recovery. He then felt a presence in the room—one that brought back a memory from his childhood.

He says, "There was no one, no one there that I could see. But it was as if there was someone in the middle of the room, because Ginny was barking. It had to be an angel. When I was young, I remember one time I was lying in my room, praying, and my mother said, 'Look, we're going to get you a dog because a dog can see angels.'"

The impossible had occurred. In spite of doctors' predictions, Philip had regained the use of his hand. But something miraculous happened to Ginny that night as well.

A few days later, while taking a walk, the dog darted away. Philip feared the worst, but when he caught up with Ginny, he found the dog licking an abandoned cat.

"I couldn't believe it," Philip says. "I'd never seen this before in my life."

Philip decided to take their new feline friend home, but this was just the beginning of Ginny's new role as guardian angel. On subsequent walks, Ginny uncovered a group of starving kittens in a drainpipe. Others were rescued near trash bins, or alone and abandoned in the fields. Ginny is always there to make them feel safe and loved. All told, Philip and Ginny have saved hundreds of cats, and found them homes.

In cases where the kittens were suffering from blindness or other physical deformities, Philip adopted them himself. He even sold some of his own possessions to care for his new pets. "I had a bunch of gold coins, and I cashed them in to feed the cats. I took my gold watches, rings, and chains and I cashed them in, 'cause I said to myself that the cats are more important."

For Philip Gonzalez, his miraculous cure, and the miracle of Ginny's uncanny ability to rescue cats, has convinced him she's a godsend.

"In Ginny," says Philip, "I see an angel, because she likes to rescue injured cats that have been abandoned. She also rescued me and was sent by God to take care of me, to watch over me."

# ELK ANGELS

The Eagles Nest wilderness area in Colorado's Rocky Mountain National Forest is known for its rugged beauty. But among search-and-rescue teams like Patti and Dan Burnett, it is also known for its dangerous and unpredictable changes of climate.

"The weather can change dramatically," Patti says. "Especially when you get above ten thousand feet. You can be on one side of the mountain, and you're headed up toward the top of the ridge and suddenly you get up top of the ridge and you see this storm coming in from a distance, and in no time at all you can be in big trouble."

In 1992, an amazing event would occur in these mountains—something even more unpredictable than the weather. Derek Potton and his young son, Ryan, had visited the mountains for a day of grouse hunting. But sometime in the morning, Ryan became separated from his father. As hours passed, the temperature fell. Derek's fear grew, for his son had been dressed in only light summer clothing.

"Right around three o'clock I decided that I better go down and get someone up here to help search."

Patti and Dan Burnett were alerted by the local sheriff's department and arrived in the remote area with their search dog, Hasty, and plenty of warm clothing. When they learned that Ryan had been dressed for summer when he disappeared, one terrifying word stuck in their minds: hypothermia.

"Hypothermia is a really insidious thing," Dan says. "People can die in the summertime as well as the winter. If your core temperature drops a few degrees, your body will shut down and you'll die."

After hours of searching, there was still no sign of Ryan. And to add to the nightmare, snow began to fall. With hope fading, the search had to be called off for the night.

"It's hard to just sit and wait," Dan says, "because all you can think about is that he's out there, lost, he's cold, and he could be dying."

The next morning, Patti and Dan were joined by another veteran tracker, Greta Sloan, and her dog, Cello.

"Cello did pick up the scent fairly quickly, I suppose," Greta remembers. "Maybe after thirty minutes. I followed him down the hill. When I got to the bottom and got within sight of him, there was Ryan. I offered him water. I gave him some food. And at that point, he was indeed at a dangerous point of hypothermia."

There was no earthly reason why this boy should have been alive, but two mysterious patches of melted snow nearby caught Greta's attention. While they waited for help to arrive, Ryan shared his miraculous story of survival.

"I was pretty scared," Ryan recalls. "I didn't know what was gonna happen, not having anyone else out there to answer me. I could hardly talk. My throat was so sore from hollering that by night I just knew I had to stop and take it easy for a while."

Terrified, alone, and freezing, Ryan knew he needed to find shelter.

"By that time, I knew I couldn't see where I was going, so I walked over to where there were some bigger trees, and there was a fir tree with branches that went almost all the way to the ground. I climbed underneath that, so that I had as much cover as I could get."

Exhausted, Ryan fell asleep. Sometime in the middle of the night, a strange noise woke him. As his eyes adjusted to the dark, he saw that there were two large elk nearby. He tried throwing sticks and pinecones to chase them away, but they kept coming back. Each time they returned, they came closer and closer. Finally, they did something that goes against the very nature of wild animals—they lay down next to the boy and stayed with him throughout the night.

"They were close enough to him all night to keep him warm," Greta says, "and that is how he survived."

Rescuers were skeptical of Ryan's story until they saw the area where the young boy had slept. The ground was thawed where two large animals had bedded down.

"He would've been dead," Dan says, "if it hadn't been for the extra heat source of two big animals lying down next to him."

Greta adds, "I believe his story is true. And one of the reasons I believe it is because it would have been totally impossible for him to have survived if it weren't."

Most parents would do anything to protect their child, and no one would call it a "miracle." But when wild animals show the same care and concern for a human child, the word "miracle" seems appropriate.

Dan says, "The time that we have on this earth is an interesting time, and it was obviously not Ryan's time to go. A miracle came to bear and that's why he is still around."

Patti adds, "I've heard of angels being disguised as humans, so I don't know why angels couldn't be disguised as elk!"

Jennifer Hill of Boulder, Colorado, is a cat lover—and she received her first cat, Hoki, under very emotional circumstances.

Jennifer says, "I inherited him when my cousin died of cancer. She actually gave him to me on her deathbed, and so I felt a very strong bond with him."

And then, in 1997, Jennifer brought home a friend for Hoki, named Lapis. But introducing the two cats wasn't that easy.

"Lapis was a small kitten and they did not get along," says Jennifer. "Hoki made it very clear that he thought she was an interloper, but over a period of about six months, she gradually won him over. So they were very close."

But at sixteen, Hoki was becoming increasingly frail.

Jennifer describes Hoki's medical problems. "For several years he had had kidney problems. And it was evolving into kidney failure. It was getting to the point where I had to give him IVs on a daily basis."

Jennifer was finally forced to make the difficult decision to put Hoki to sleep. "Right before I took Hoki to the vet, I brought Lapis and Hoki together to say good-bye, because I thought it was only fair that they should be able to say good-bye. And they touched noses through the cage, and then I took him," says Jennifer.

"When I came back from the doctor that day, I brought the cage in and I actually told Lapis that Hoki had passed. And when I did that, she went to the cage and she licked the cage and sniffed at it . . . and I felt like she understood."

Later that day, Jennifer decided to let Lapis spend some time outdoors, something she did every day. But this time Lapis didn't return.

Jennifer repeatedly called her cat, but to no avail. "I wanted to bring her in and I didn't see her and then it got to be dusk. I started worrying right away. I always let her out during the day, but brought her back in at night because there are coyotes in the area."

By now, night had fallen, and Lapis had still not returned. "I started worrying, because of what had happened that day, and because it just wasn't like her not to show up. I was worried that she was grieving Hoki. I was worried that maybe she was angry with me.

"That night I started putting posters together. The next day I started putting posters up in the area. I ran around answering calls of people who had seen a black-and-white cat," Jennifer remembers. "And many people saw black-and-white cats. But they were all not her."

Jennifer continued to drive around her neighborhood, desperately looking for Lapis. Unfortunately, she was looking in all the wrong places. After two months of canvassing her neighborhood with posters and speaking with anyone who might have seen her lost cat, Jennifer lost all hope of ever finding Lapis.

She says, "It got discouraging when time after time, it was the wrong cat or the cat wasn't there. And I was getting discouraged and frustrated."

But nearly three thousand miles away in the Canadian Yukon, two men were about to make an incredible discovery. As Ed Chambers and his brother-in-law Roy checked out an old truck for parts, something else caught their attention.

"We were standing there looking at this axle and talking about it," says Ed, "and my dog, Bee Vee, came right along behind us. She had stopped underneath this tree and started barking. So I walked back to look. I thought maybe she had a squirrel, because she likes chasing squirrels."

But when Ed got to the tree, he quickly saw that this was no squirrel. He explains, "I looked up, and about ten feet up in the tree, here's this black cat sitting there, all scrunched up on a limb, looking down at the dog."

Ed could tell immediately that it was a house cat. "As far as I could tell," he says, "it was in excellent condition. It wasn't starving or anything. It was quite agile to get up that tree ahead of my dog.

"But in the meantime, I looked up in the tree again and the cat's gone."

About a week later, Ed's dog spotted the cat again. He recalls, "I walked out of the shop, and my dog is out barking behind another shed there. So I went back in the shop and got my .22 because I thought it was a squirrel.

"I walked back behind the shop, and there's my dog again underneath another big tree. And the same cat, with a nice, big, bright green collar on its neck, is sitting up there on the limb looking down on us. The cat was safe."

When he arrived home, Ed mentioned the cat to his niece Susan.

Says Ed, "We get to talking about this cat. 'Oh, yeah,' she says. 'This is a real friendly cat. I just opened the door and the cat came right in and made itself at home, and I fed it.' Susan was the only one who could get the cat to come to her."

Four nights later, Ed's son-in-law David Grant was visiting. Once again, the subject of the mysterious and friendly black-and-white cat came up. Susan told them, "I got the collar off. It's in my bag."

When David and Susan looked at the tag on the collar, they saw that it had a phone number on it. David recalls that "it had the cat's name, Lapis, and a phone number. So we looked up the area code and saw that it was Colorado. I phoned the number and nobody was home—a voice mail came on."

But Jennifer actually was home when that call came in. "At one o'clock in the morning, my phone rang. I was half-asleep, and I just let the answering machine get it. I heard a male voice, and then I heard laughter in the background. And I thought, Well, maybe it's somebody at a party, you know, calling the wrong number."

But something made Jennifer play back the message on her answering machine.

Jennifer says, "The message said something along the lines of 'We've got your cat. We're in the Yukon. We'll call you back.' At first I just couldn't believe it. I thought it was a prank, because I had posted my number all over town.

"But then I looked, and I have caller ID, and I saw that the number on the caller ID had an area code that was unfamiliar to me."

Jennifer called an operator to check the area code, and discovered that it was indeed for the Yukon.

"I thought, This is just strange," Jennifer continues. "I might as well, what do I have to lose? So I called back."

Jennifer called the number, and David answered, telling her that her cat was with him in Champagne, Yukon. But Jennifer still wasn't convinced. "I had had so many of these experiences that I had a list of screening questions. I asked about the specific markings and specific coat on her, and specific coloration of her tag and collar. But all of David's answers were checking out perfectly."

Jennifer admits, "About halfway through, I started to believe that it really was her. I said to him, 'Is she okay?' and he said, 'The cat's fine. A little skinny.'"

Ed said, "I couldn't imagine how that cat could get here. I didn't really believe the cat had come from Colorado."

Jennifer thanked them and arranged to retrieve Lapis as

soon as possible, amazed that her beloved pet was safe at last.

And she continued to be amazed when, several days later and two months after she disappeared, Lapis arrived home from the Yukon.

Says Jennifer, "In a way, I just couldn't believe it was her, even though I knew it was her. There was a moment of recognition and simultaneous misrecognition, because she looked different. She was smaller and thinner and I could tell she had been through a lot. But I was also very happy. I was overwhelmingly happy."

After Lapis had once again settled into her domestic routine, Jennifer tried to piece together what must have happened. She explains, "I found out that some of my neighbors were actually loading up furniture to move to their house in Alaska, and that some of the neighborhood cats had been playing in the back of the trailer."

Apparently, Lapis was inside the trailer when the moving men were ready to go. Jennifer says, "I can only imagine that she must have been pretty frightened in the trailer. Maybe not at first, but after a while when she couldn't get out and there was, I'm sure, no food or water for her."

Thousands of miles later, when Lapis arrived in the Yukon, she had to face many challenges that could have taken her life.

As Ed Chambers explains, "This was in the springtime. This wasn't in the dead of summer or anything. It was cold at night."

And David Grant agrees that Lapis was facing an uphill

battle. "It had a lot going against it—like coyotes and foxes and other little animals that would prey on the cat. There would probably be more things trying to eat it than it had to eat."

But miraculously, Lapis avoided the many dangers of the cold and forbidding Yukon Territory. And thanks to an identification tag and the kindness of strangers, she finally found her way home. Truly, it was an incredible journey.

Jennifer Hill sums it up with a laugh. "My explanation of this amazing event happening, that a cat goes missing and travels three thousand miles away and then is reunited with its owner? It seems pretty miraculous to me."

"I couldn't imagine how this cat could get here. I don't imagine it would happen again in my lifetime," marvels Ed.

And for David Grant, "I'm just real happy to see her get her cat back, because I know some people get really attached to their animals."

As Jennifer reflects on the miraculous return of her pet, she says, "Now that I've gotten Lapis back, I feel like the people in the Yukon who helped me out were great. They did a lot for someone they didn't even know. If David Grant and Edward Chambers were here right now, I would hug them both and say thank you. And take them out to dinner."

# BULLETPROOF DOG

On the night of April 19, 1996, Kendal Plank's house in Tucson, Arizona, was the scene of a terrifying home invasion.

Kendal was alone that night, sleeping. Her husband, Jerry, was working the midnight shift in a local copper mine. It was just after one A.M. when her nightmare began.

"I woke up all of a sudden to all of the dogs in the neighborhood just going berserk," recalls Kendal. "I really didn't think much about it, because it was just dogs barking. Next thing I knew, I heard footsteps in the gravel in front of my house. And he went to the door and jiggled the handle.

"The next thing I remember was someone tapping at

the bathroom window," she says. "I don't think he thought anyone was home. He was making too much noise. So I called 911."

Kendal told the 911 dispatcher that she could hear someone trying to break into her house.

"They got the information from me, but I did something to the phone where I couldn't hear them anymore," she says, "so I called my sister-in-law, Sandy. She lives up the street from us."

"Sandy, someone's breaking into the house," she told her.

Sandy woke up her husband, and told him to go over to Kendal's.

"Tell him to hurry," said Kendal.

Kendal's English springer spaniel, Brandy, stayed close by her side, sensing that something was terribly wrong.

"She just kept looking at my face, my eyes. And she was like 'What's going on, Mom?'" says Kendal. "And all I could say was 'Oh, God.' The whole time. 'Oh, God.' I could hear him tapping at this window the whole time."

Still on the phone with her sister-in-law, Kendal paced inside, waiting for help. "I wanted to go out the front door," she says, "but I didn't know how many were out there, and I was afraid that if I opened up the garage door, they'd shoot me or they'd catch me or something. So I was trapped in the house.

"All of a sudden, I heard this crash," Kendal recalls.

"Sandy, he's in the house!" she exclaimed.

"And then my panic really started going berserk, because I didn't know where he was. He was just down the hall!"

And then, the house became deadly quiet.

"Then all of a sudden, I see this 9mm machine gun," Kendal says. "It was like, Oh my gosh, this is it. And he turned to me, military style, put the gun on his hip, and shot me. Shot me twice."

Her sister-in-law heard the gunshots through the phone, and asked her what had happened. "Sandy, oh, my God, he shot me," Kendal said.

Before he could fire again, Brandy turned on the intruder. The dog lunged, and clamped down on the intruder's arm, but the English springer spaniel was no match for a machine gun. The intruder shot at the dog repeatedly. Finally, shaking him free, the man jumped back out the bathroom window he'd come through.

Before the shooting ended, the police had arrived at the house.

"The officer heard what he believed was two shots being fired," describes Deputy Egurrola. "The suspect pointed the weapon at the officers, and three officers shot and fired, and killed the suspect."

During all of the commotion, Brandy managed to make her way back to where Kendal had fallen.

"And she's sitting there, you know, with a happy face," says Kendal. "She's just got a little bit of blood on her white chest, and she's like, 'Okay Mom, the intruder's gone, I'm here.'

"But little did I know," she says, "that she had taken five bullets. And they had gone clean through her. Each one."

When the officers entered the home, they found Kendal on the floor and Brandy lifeless nearby.

"The dog was in the living room," recalls Deputy Egurrola, "and there was a large amount of blood around the animal."

The dog was presumed dead, and officers focused all of their attention on saving Kendal's life.

Jerry learned about his wife's ordeal after she'd been taken to a local hospital.

"They told me that my house got broken into, and my wife got shot, and my dog got shot. I was told by one deputy that the dog was dead," says Jerry.

But they were wrong.

A canine officer noticed that the dog was still breathing, and they rushed Brandy to a veterinary operating room. Miraculously, after being shot point-blank five times, she survived. But the terror of that night stayed with her.

"For almost a year, she slept underneath the bathroom window that the intruder came into," says Kendal.

"When Kendal's having a nightmare, Brandy gets up from where she's lying at, goes over, and lays her head across Kendal's throat, to make sure everything's all right," adds Jerry.

"I feel safe with her," says Kendal. "She's become quite my hero, and my husband's hero."

"If Brandy wasn't there, I think my wife would have been dead," agrees Jerry. "I've heard from one of the deputies that there were bite wounds on the guy's arm. I believe that she took a few good bites at him, you know?"

"If the dog hadn't been there, things would have been very different," confirms Deputy Egurrola. "I would have been investigating a homicide, instead of just an officer-involved shooting.

"We, together as a unit, decided that we would like to show some kind of gratitude toward the dog for making our job a little bit easier," he says. "We presented the dog with a citation of bravery."

"The sheriff's department designed the first Purple Heart for a canine, and presented it," says Kendal. "She saved my life. If I hadn't had Brandy, I believe the intruder would have made sure I was dead. But Brandy was there with me. She never left my side.

"I believe you have angels. You have guardian angels," adds Kendal. "Brandy took five bullets for me and lived. . . . I believe that's a miracle."

## $\mathcal{C}$AT FINDS GAS LEAK

In the summer of 1995, the Bowling Green, Ohio, home of Ray and Carol Steiner was a hospital ward. Ray spent his days on the couch, recuperating from a triple bypass operation, and his wife, Carol, was confined to a hospital bed, recovering from foot surgery. Both of them were sleeping nearly nineteen hours a day.

"It was incredible. We would get up, eat, and go back to sleep," remembers Carol. "And then we would get hungry again, eat, and go back to sleep."

"That summer was extremely hot, and we'd had the house locked up with the air-conditioning on," says Ray. "We were both very tired, had headaches, high blood pressure, loss of memory . . . and neither of us could figure out why."

"The doctor kept saying it was postoperative fatigue," adds Carol.

The Steiners' constant companion through all of this was a red tabby cat that Carol had rescued as a kitten.

"I saw someone getting rid of a bunch of kittens and a mother cat, and it was obvious that they were going to be thrown in a field," she recalls. "So I just reached in, grabbed a piece of red fluff, and I brought it home."

The kitten had never meowed. When he wanted to enter or leave the house, he would drum on the door with his paws—so they named him Ringo.

And then one morning as Ray was napping and Carol was reading a book, she heard a loud knock at the front door. But when she went to answer it, she found Ringo sitting there. Apparently, he'd thrown himself against the door.

"And so I thought, Jeez, he must really want to go outside," Carol says. "But when I opened the door, he wouldn't go out. He just stood there in the foyer. I said, 'Kitty, let's go out.' And he just looked at me."

Ringo had never acted like this before, but Carol was too tired to wait for him to make up his mind.

"It was very, very frustrating," she says. Finally, she pulled the cat inside, shut the door, and went back to bed. "I went back, got my leg up, just got relaxed for a minute, and *wham!* He threw himself at the door again."

The cat was beginning to try her patience, but it was obvious that he wanted something, so Carol struggled back to the front door on her crutches. But once again, Ringo positioned himself on the threshold, and wouldn't move.

"I tried to push him out with my crutch," Carol recalls.

"I was really kind of giving him a good *oomph,* as much as I could, but he just got really, really stubborn about the whole thing, and he just stood there. I said, 'Well, come back in, or go out,' and he just stood there, that was it."

Finally, Carol says, "I opened the door a little farther, and when Ringo saw me give a movement like I might come out, he stepped onto the porch. And then he turned over his shoulder and he kept giving me a high meow."

It was the first time that Carol had ever heard Ringo make a sound, but when she approached him to find out what he wanted, he moved away. It was as if he was trying to get her to follow him . . . so she did.

Ringo led Carol out of the house and around to the side yard, pausing to wait for her to catch up, and peering back at her expectantly.

"He would go just a few feet and wait for old clunky to catch up to him, and then he would look over his shoulder again," explains Carol. "He would make sure that I was there, and I said, 'Okay, I'm coming, I'm coming.' He carefully led me all the way around to the right side of our house. And I thought, Boy, I wonder what he's doing on this side of the house? This is unusual."

At first, Carol thought Ringo was leading her to a dead bird, but then he stopped at a pile of rocks, and began pawing the ground like a dog.

"He started digging in our lava landscaping," says Carol. "And he was actually getting bloody feet over it, trying to dig down into the landscaping."

Recognizing that Ringo was desperately trying to show

her something, Carol moved toward the place he was digging . . . and that's when it hit her.

"It's gas!" she realized.

"It was almost as pungent as if you would turn on a gas stove and wait for about fifteen to twenty seconds. It was really that strong," Carol explains. "All of a sudden I was awake. I didn't hurt. I had an adrenaline rush. And the first thing I yelled was, 'Ray, we have a gas leak!'"

They immediately called the gas company and a serviceman was sent to the home.

"And so he said, 'Oh, don't worry, Mrs. Steiner. I'm sure it's absolutely nothing,'" says Carol.

She followed the gas repairman back along the side of the house, still hobbling on her crutches. He tested the gas meter for leaks, but no bubbles appeared, which meant that the system was safe.

"He turned around and he said, 'Mrs. Steiner, look. The gas meter's perfect. There's no gas leak,'" recalls Carol.

Carol wasn't reassured, however, and she directed him to test the area where Ringo had been digging.

"He just basically was like 'Let's humor the lady,' but he took his hand meter and extended it out, and it immediately registered right to the top of that meter," she says. An alarm started blaring.

"I think he was totally surprised, totally astonished, and he certainly became quite pale. His reaction to the whole thing was, 'Oh, my God, we really have a bad gas leak, and I've got to get to the truck,'" says Carol. Still, as the repairman made a call, he told her not to worry, that everything would be fine.

It turned out that the leak was so large that the slightest exposure to a spark would have caused a disaster.

"If the gas had ignited, our house would have gone first, quickly followed by all the homes that would have been linked with us. And so six to eight homes would have blown up simultaneously," reveals Carol.

Ringo saved more than twenty lives from going up in a ball of flame. It turned out that methane had been leaking from a crack in the gas main and accumulating in the Steiners' house, which had been shut tight against the heat. The Steiners, suffering from all the symptoms of methane poisoning, were on the verge of dying from it.

Eventually, Ringo received national recognition for his lifesaving efforts.

"Ringo was given the Stillman Award from the American Humane Association, because they felt that he interceded with bravery and saved our lives, and many other lives," says Carol.

"I believe there was a miracle here," states Ray. "Cats, as has been said many times, aren't known to do such things, and Ringo saving our lives is indeed a miracle."

"I do believe that there are angels around, and I think they use whatever method they can to take care of people," adds Carol. "I believe a guardian angel did step in, and the method that the guardian angel used was Ringo.

"He saved our lives," she says. "There's no question about it. This kitty saved the day."

# THE ULTIMATE GIFT

#  Adopted Kidney

In 1976, Shirley Armstead was a happily married wife and mother of two sons. But Shirley had always dreamed of having a daughter. To ensure that she got one, Shirley decided to adopt.

Originally from Louisiana, Shirley came from a Creole background, and was looking for a mixed-race child.

"My father is part Jewish and French," says Shirley, "and my mother is also French. That's why I wanted to have a daughter that would blend into our family."

Because Shirley's request was so specific, the adoption agency was able to produce only one candidate—a three-year-old child named Dana.

The social worker gave Shirley a file and photo, and asked her to take a look.

"It looked so much like my little boy," recalls Shirley, "and she said, 'It's not, it's your little girl. It's the daughter that I have for you,' and I was like 'I can't believe it. They look so much alike.'"

The little girl lived in foster care three hundred miles away from the Armsteads' Los Angeles home. And as Shirley and her two sons arrived to meet Dana for the first time, they were filled with both apprehension and anticipation.

Shirley had her heart set on adopting this child. But would the little girl be open and willing to accept them as her family? It didn't take long to learn the answer.

Shirley's oldest son, Derek, still remembers his first impressions.

"She was lovable," he says. "She had a big smile on her face. She looked very happy."

For Shirley, the moment she knew that Dana was the daughter she'd always dreamed of came from a simple childlike question.

"She kind of won me over when she said, 'When we get to my new home, would you please buy me some shoes?'" recalls Shirley. "And I thought, That's my little girl. . . . She likes to shop. That was it."

The decision had been made, and four Armsteads would be returning on the long drive home to Los Angeles.

"We made a family," says Shirley. "It was good to have this third child in my life to care for and to love."

In the years that followed, it became clear that the Armstead family was where Dana belonged. She may not have been blood-related, but in her heart, and in the hearts of her parents and brothers, she was an Armstead.

"I think that's where the miracle started," says Dana, "that I was brought into a home and given the love and the care that I needed."

And then in 1994, tragedy struck. Dana's older brother Derek was diagnosed with a fatal illness.

"I have chronic kidney failure coming from hypertension," explains Derek. "It is very deadly. You can die overnight. You can die in a week. You can die in six months."

Drugs and dialysis provided temporary relief, but what Derek really needed was a new kidney. And that could take years.

"I was afraid for his life, because I knew that he needed a donor and that he was on the transplant list," says Dana, "and there's gotta be thousands and thousands of people waiting on transplants. What is the likelihood of him getting one?"

"I was more afraid for my kids, because they needed somebody to guide them through life," says Derek, "to show them what was right and what was wrong, and I wanted to be there for them."

Throughout his ordeal, the Armsteads banded together, trying to bolster Derek's spirits, while knowing that none of his blood relatives had tested positive as a kidney donor.

His mother put on a brave face, but inside, the thought of losing her son was unbearable.

"I felt like dying myself," Shirley says. "I felt like, that's it, I just didn't want to deal with the reality. There was no talk about a possible outside donor. It was almost as if it was a shut case."

Time was running out, and even Derek had given up all hope.

"I had just gotten to the point where I was really, really depressed," admits Derek, "and was just ready to give up because I saw no hope."

Dana was particularly concerned about her older brother.

"I'm gonna go and get tested," she told him. "What do you think about that?"

"I think you're crazy," Derek responded.

Derek had always told her that because she was not a blood relative, the odds of being a match were a long shot, and she should save herself the trouble. But time was running out, and Dana decided she had nothing to lose.

"I just said, 'Wouldn't that be funny if I was a match?'" recalls Dana, "and he said, 'Yeah, right' and that was it. It was left at that."

"And when she told me she was going to go down and be tested, I just really didn't think much of it," says Derek. "I was like, yeah, whatever. You know, go for it."

And she did. The first step was blood-screen testing for kidney compatibility. Knowing that the odds of matching her adopted brother's kidneys were very slim, Dana turned to prayer.

"As I was going through the testing, I was hoping inside, Oh, God, I hope everything works out fine. I hope I can help him," says Dana. "I would go home and I would say, Dear God, please help me to be able to help Derek. I really want my nephews to be able to grow up and have a father in their lives. I don't feel this is something that Derek deserves.... Please continue to bless me to be able to help him."

After a battery of additional blood and tissue tests, Dana received the news she'd been praying for.

"First I called my mom and said, 'You're not going to believe this.' She said, 'What?'" recalls Dana. "I said, 'I'm a match. Can you believe it? I can donate a kidney to Derek. I feel so happy.'"

"I was speechless," says Shirley. "I didn't say anything. I was choked up; I couldn't say anything."

"And then she said, 'You have got to be kidding.' I could hear the joy in her voice, like she was on the verge of tears," says Dana. "She said, 'Now, isn't that ironic, that we would pick you twenty-three years ago out of a foster home, and you would turn out to be the person that could save Derek's life.'"

When she told her brother, he also couldn't believe the news.

"You're kidding, right?" he said.

"He laughed it off," says Dana. "I said, 'No, we are a match and I can give you a kidney, so don't chicken out now.'"

"My whole life changed," declares Derek, "because I saw a chance to give my kids a better life, let them enjoy some of the things in life that I did when I was growing up. I just felt a whole lot of hope at that point."

On March 31, 1999, Derek and Dana checked into the

UCLA Medical Center. Transplant day had finally arrived, and a camera crew from *It's a Miracle* was there to document it, and speak with Dr. Albin Gritsch.

"Both of them are relatively young and healthy, so their blood and their tissues should be in good condition," stated Dr. Gritsch. "I don't have any concerns that they will have problems with the operation at this time."

As medical technicians prepared them for the operation, Derek and Dana were flooded with mixed emotions, but mostly relieved that the transplant was finally going forward.

"I'm gonna wake up and be a whole new person," Derek claimed.

"He just asked me if I was sure that I wanted to still do this, that I could still chicken out; it's my last chance," Dana laughs.

"I'm fine. I'm staying. It's a go," she told him.

Dana was the first to go under the knife, and almost immediately there were complications. Her mother waited anxiously in the hall.

"I'm nervous right now," she said. "We've waited for so long for this to happen. This is it. My heart is like *bumpeta-bumpeta-bumpeta,* really anxious. I want it to be over."

After nearly three hours and the removal of two ribs, the doctors were finally able to extract Dana's left kidney.

"Here's the kidney," said Dr. Gritsch. "We're going to take it next door. It's all ready to go."

Shirley and the rest of the family waited nervously as the kidney was transplanted into Derek.

"I'm hoping that everything will work out for both of them, especially Derek," said Shirley. "Because if it doesn't, we know what the end result will be. He will die."

Four hours after the surgery began, the Armstead family was given the news they'd been waiting for.

"Everything went just fine with both operations," the doctor told them. "They're both in the recovery room. You'll be able to see them up there."

It was a joyful moment for the Armstead family, who can only wonder at the remarkable sequence of events that gave Derek a new chance at life.

"I definitely believe it's a miracle," says Dana. "For some reason, my picture was the only one that was given to them. They chose me."

"I feel very strongly that a miracle took place," agrees Shirley. "When God put that little girl in my life twenty-three years ago, I had no other children to chose from, only that one. There wasn't a question. It was like 'She's yours.'"

"I believe that she's my guardian angel," says Derek, "that she was sent here from God twenty-three years ago and he made it possible that we were a match, so that she could do this for me."

**L**UCKY LAYOVER

For Janet Larson, Northwest Flight 1815 was a journey that might mean the difference between life and death. Her sister, Deborah, had suffered from liver disease for the last ten years. But now, her kidneys were failing.

"She was sick all the time," recalls Janet. "She spent an average of ten months every year in the hospital. And when she wasn't in the hospital, she was home in bed. She had no quality of life whatsoever. It's a very heartrending process to go through, to watch someone very close to you fade before your eyes."

Janet was flying to New Orleans to donate one of her own kidneys to buy her sister some time. But ultimately, Deborah would need a new liver to survive.

Janet planned on using the flight time to educate herself on the transplant operation ahead of her.

"I Xeroxed everything I could find on kidney anatomy and physiology," Janet says, "so I could study it on the plane and just kind of update myself on how the kidney functions, so that I could ask intelligent questions of the doctors."

The flight was full. Only one seat remained empty at takeoff time. It was the seat next to Janet. But at the last minute, a man named Allen Van Meter boarded the aircraft to claim it.

Like Janet, Allen was also on his way to see a family member. A tragic accident had left his twenty-five-year-old nephew, Michael Gibson, brain-dead and on life support. Allen was going to be with his grieving sister.

"Michael was alive, but it looked bad," says Allen. "When I boarded the plane, I'd pretty well decided I wasn't going to have a conversation with anybody. You know, I was just going to try to work some of this out in my head to get some understanding."

Still, Allen couldn't help but notice the pictures and medical charts spread out on Janet's lap.

"Are you a doctor?" Allen asked.

"And I told him the story and why I was flying to be with Debbie," Janet says. "And he said, 'I'm going to see my sister, too, but for a very different reason.'"

"I said, 'Yeah, I'm going to Paducah, Kentucky, because my nephew just accidentally shot himself and his condition is looking real bad. They don't think he's going to live,'" Allen says.

Because of Michael's hopeless condition, Allen had helped convince his sister to donate the young man's organs.

"And I said, 'Well, God bless you, sir,'" continues Janet. "'I wish there were more people like you, because then nobody would have to wait, and nobody would have to suffer.' And I went back to studying my diagram."

But moments later, Allen made an astonishing suggestion.

"I tapped her on the shoulder, and I said, 'How about Michael's liver? We'll use that for your sister.' Like that. And she looked at me like I was a nut," Allen remembers.

"I really appreciate the offer," Janet replied, "but I don't think they'll let us do that. It's a whole lot more complicated than that." She adds, "And a couple minutes later, he tapped me on the shoulder again."

Allen explains, "I had a sense of urgency that I needed to push this. And I said, 'We need to make some calls and find out what we need to do.'"

After learning that Allen's nephew and Debbie shared the same blood type, Janet got through to Memorial Medical Mid-City Campus in New Orleans.

"He's brain-dead," Janet told the nurse. "We've got him on life support. And what we want to know is if we can get his nephew's liver for my sister. Is that possible?

"And she said, 'Is he the same blood type?' and I said, 'Yes, ma'am, we've already checked on that.' And she said, 'Yes, you can.' Just like that. It was so powerful, and I said, 'Tell me what to do.'"

The nurse instructed them to call Michael's hospital in Springfield, Missouri, and explain the situation.

"We want to donate his liver to Deborah White," Allen told Michael's nurse. "And she said, 'Mr. Van Meter, it's too late. They've already unhooked him.' There was a big pause, like she had set down the phone and left, and she came back and she said, 'No, Mr. Van Meter. It's not too late. I just stopped it.' That's how close it was."

While these two perfect strangers worked together to make a miracle happen thirty thousand feet in the air, on the ground, phone calls flew between hospitals. Dr. Philip Boudreaux was Deborah's physician.

"I received a phone call from The Organ Procurement Agency in the Missouri area," says Dr. Boudreaux, "informing us that we had a liver offer for our patient, Deborah White. And, of course, I was flabbergasted and pleased. But I thought the probability of this proceeding any further than an interesting phone call was very slim."

With time of the essence, Dr. Boudreaux moved into action, sending a transplant surgeon to Springfield while scheduling Deborah's operation in New Orleans. Meanwhile, in the air, Janet placed the most important call of the day: to her sister.

"I was very emotional at this point," Janet recalls, "and thinking, Oh, my God, this could happen, oh, my God, this could happen. I said, 'Listen carefully, honey. Don't get too excited, but I think I may have found you a liver.' "

"I was trying not to be excited," remembers Debbie White. "I was trying to just be calm about it because it was an impossibility. I mean, I have a better chance of winning the lottery."

By the time their plane landed in Memphis, Tennessee,

Allen and Janet had formed an incredible bond. And they bid each other an emotional good-bye.

"I said, 'Well, everything's gonna be fine. You watch and see.' And I watched her and everything," says Allen. "Every few steps she would turn and wave again, you know. It was good stuff."

For the two sisters, a joyful reunion in New Orleans and a day of waiting began.

"The whole day was pitted with ups and downs," says Janet, "and ups and downs, and ups and downs."

"I called my transplant coordinator and said, 'Okay, tell me I'm crazy, tell me this is not a go,' you know. That's really what I expected to hear. And she confirmed the fact that I am crazy," laughs Deborah, "but that this thing just might work out."

Finally, after hours of waiting, the phone rang. But it wasn't the call they'd been hoping for.

Janet explains, "The transplant coordinator said, 'I'm sorry, this isn't going to happen. The last plane has left Missouri, and there is no way that they're going to wait for the organ. So there's no way for us to get this organ to you.' "

"My transplant coordinator said, 'Don't give up,' " continues Deborah. " 'I know you better than that.' She said, 'Give me forty-five minutes.' And that was probably the longest forty-five minutes of my life."

Another phone call brought the incredible news that during that time, the hospital had managed to charter a jet to pick up the liver from Springfield. And four hours later, Deborah was being prepped for surgery.

"I knew there was no turning back," says Deborah. "I knew everything was going to be okay. And I was the happiest person in the world."

At 11:30 P.M., doctors began the delicate transplant operation. It took less than half the time expected and was a complete success. Even more amazing, Deborah was home in just eight days. But the miracle didn't end there. The liver was such a perfect match that, so far, Deborah hasn't needed Janet's kidney.

"I'm still in recovery, but getting better every day," explains Deborah. "I was pretty positive before. I've appreciated the little things in life, but now it's so much more intense. Every little moment, every little thing, I get excited about, and I'm really glad to be here."

But even in their great joy, Janet and Deborah will never forget the sacrifice made by Michael Gibson.

"I mourn Michael's death," Deborah says, "but in a way, he lives on. He saved my life. He lives on with . . . in me."

Dr. Boudreaux adds, "This miracle, if you will, happened because someone in their moment of tragedy decided to do something for the greater good."

"We feel very strongly," adds Janet, "that we were given this miracle so that Debbie can use this special story to promote organ donation, and to save other people's lives with it."

"I think potential donors can hold their heads really high," concludes Deborah, "because they're the heroes walking around. They're gonna save lives and that's the ultimate gift. It's priceless."

# HEART FROM A FRIEND

In January of 1993, thirty-six-year-old Rodney Debaun was the epitome of good health.

"I was 155 pounds, and I could bench press 275, and I was playing in three basketball leagues a week," says Rodney. "I didn't smoke; I didn't drink. I was guaranteed to live to be ninety years old."

And then, a month later, Rodney became ill.

"I was pretty sick for a couple of days," he remembers. "I just had flu symptoms. In a few days I was feeling better, and I went back to playing basketball. But my endurance just didn't seem quite the same. I couldn't run down the basketball court for more than about four or five minutes without needing to come out."

By the end of the basketball season, Rodney's health was deteriorating rapidly, and his wife, Isabel, was deeply concerned.

She recalls, "When he would lie down, he felt like he had pressure on his chest. He told me, 'I just can't lie down. I have to go sleep in the recliner.' That was when I finally said, 'Let's get to the doctor. This is not normal.'"

Rodney was referred to a cardiologist and, after a series of tests, received some shocking news.

His doctor told him, "What you have is a cardiomyopathy. Basically, what that is is heart failure."

Rodney remembers, "I couldn't imagine what he was talking about. I asked him, 'What does all that mean? I mean, on a scale of one to ten, where am I?' And I thought he was gonna say, 'Well, you're a six or a seven.' You can fix a six or a seven."

But the doctor told him, "Optimistically, maybe a two." He said that Rodney had lost 88% of his heart.

He then asked his doctor, "What do we do to fix it?" Rodney says, "I've always been an eternal optimist. And I wasn't prepared for the next answer."

His doctor replied, "I wish I could say we could do something, but we can't."

"He said the only thing we could do is a heart transplant," Rodney recalls. "In my wildest imagination I wouldn't dream that two hours later I was gonna be told I need a heart transplant."

The doctor referred Rodney to one of the top heart transplant specialists in the United States, Dr. Lonnie Whiddon.

Dr. Whiddon explains, "He had a poor outlook in terms of survival. We were concerned about whether he would survive even a few months. The chances of getting a donor organ in a few months' time are not good. Many people wait for a year or longer for an appropriate or suitable donor organ for heart transplantation."

Rodney was given only six months to live, but his heart could stop functioning at any moment, without any warning.

"I went to bed every night not knowing if I was going to wake up, literally," says Rodney. "And subconsciously, I think I put off going to sleep because of that."

Isabel remembers, "My time to cry was in the shower, because I knew the boys couldn't see me, and I wouldn't upset them. But there were a few times they would catch me, and I would be back there crying and trying to accept it."

"Isabel came to me one morning and said that I probably needed to have a more in-depth talk with Heath, our oldest son," says Rodney.

Isabel says, "He asked me if his dad was going to die. . . . I didn't know what to tell him."

"To sit down with your eleven-year-old son, and look him in the eye, and say, 'I might not be here'—that was probably one of the hardest things I've ever had to do.

"So that night, about midnight, I decided to seek some help, and I didn't know where to look for it. I hadn't read the Bible much in my life, and I just let it fall open. It fell open to a page in Psalms that said, 'My heart fails within me, and show me the number of my days, and man at his best is just a whisper.' And I said, 'God, if you'll let me be here, I'll give up everything that I'm doing and devote the rest of my life to whatever you want. Just give me my life back.'"

Rodney's prayer that night would soon be answered in a miraculous and unexpected way. The very next day, he received a phone call from his friend Ken Johnson, who had a sign of his own.

Rodney remembers, "He said, 'Rodney, I woke up this morning and I was told I was going to find you a heart.' I said, 'Well, okay, I'll take the help, but I don't know what you can do.' He knew that God wanted him to do something."

Soon after his phone call, Ken began stopping by to see Rodney. On one of these visits, he brought along a friend, "Lucky" William Bramlett.

Lucky recalls, "The first time I met Rodney, his skin was pale and he was very weak. He didn't look real good."

"I was in a situation where even having conversation was tiring," says Rodney. "Ken and Mr. Bramlett stayed for a couple of hours and then they left."

It was a short visit—nothing profound was discussed—and yet it was a meeting that would deeply affect both Rodney and Lucky Bramlett's lives.

Several weeks later, Lucky's grandson, David Nicklas, was involved in a serious motorcycle accident that left him brain-dead with no hope of recovery. That same night, Lucky experienced an extraordinary calling.

Lucky explains, "I was lying there, really heartbroken over my grandson. And all of a sudden, I just stopped, and I told my wife that I knew somebody who needs that heart."

Lucky's astounding resolution to donate his grandson's heart to Rodney was accepted by the entire Nicklas family. Rodney was astonished by their generosity.

"I didn't know what to say," remembers Rodney. "I felt terrible for the Nicklas family, but at the same time I realized instantly that I might not be leaving my kids."

It was amazing news for Rodney and his family. But before Dr. Whiddon could perform the operation, David's heart would have to pass a series of tests to confirm that it was actually suitable for transplantation.

Dr. Whiddon recalls, "I tried to reassure Rodney and also comfort him, but to expect maybe that things wouldn't work out. There are a lot of variables that go into this. The organ may not be suitable for donation, there may be problems with blood studies or compatibility that would make the transplant unlikely."

It was a stormy night in October when the Debaun family received the call they'd been waiting for.

"Immediately I knew, well, that's it. That's the hospital. Ruth Button, who was the Transplant Coordinator at this hospital, said, 'Rodney, how quickly can you get to the hospital?' I said, 'thirty minutes.' And she said, 'Well, come on in. We're going to try a transplant.'"

Later that night, Dr. Whiddon retrieved David Nicklas's healthy heart and in the wee hours of the next morning, he transplanted it into Rodney's chest. Rodney made a miraculous recovery, and was released from the medical center just nine days after the transplant.

"He ran a marathon soon after his operation," says Dr.

Whiddon. "That was quite remarkable to all of us. I have seen things that make me believe that people with strong faith usually come through these things better than those without strong faith."

In 1996, Rodney decided to share his miracle with others by establishing The David Nicklas Organ Donor Awareness Foundation. David's sister, Becky Nicklas, works alongside Rodney on a daily basis.

"I get to spend every day with him," says Becky. "And that in itself is amazing—to be able to see him and to know that David's heart is inside there. If I need a little bit of my brother, I know all I have to do is go up to Rodney and feel his chest, and there's a precious heartbeat there that's David."

"The Nicklas family is the most remarkable family in the entire world," says Rodney. "David's mom and dad and me, we're together all the time. We go on vacations together. Every second they see me, they know that I'm here and their son's not.

"I realize that when you wake up in the morning, you've been given a gift. I have two wonderful kids, and the best wife in the world. I do owe my life to a miracle. Absolutely."

# THE NICHOLAS EFFECT

In 1989, Reginald Green, a former reporter for some of Britain's major newspapers, and his wife, Maggie, moved their family to Bodega Bay, California. There, they raised their son, Nicholas, and daughter, Eleanor, in a peaceful home overlooking the ocean. Summers, however, were spent traveling in Europe.

"Oh, we loved it; we all loved it. The buildings, the history of it," says Reg. "Nicholas loved those sorts of things too."

It was 1994, and that year the Greens were vacationing in southern Italy.

"It was the first time that, as a family, we had been south of Rome, really," recalls Maggie. "So, we were driving down from there, seeing some sights along the way, and then looking forward to about a week in Sicily."

To reach Sicily, they would have to drive through a region called Calabria.

"We didn't know that that stretch of the road was dangerous," says Maggie. "You know, Calabria had an ancient reputation as a place for bandits. But I didn't know that it was still a place of bandits."

At about 10:30 P.M., Reg was driving a deserted stretch of road with the rest of his family asleep in the car, when suddenly a car approached from behind and pulled up next to him.

At this point, Maggie woke up. "I looked across and saw a man with a mask and a gun. They were shouting," she says. "We don't know what the words were, but it was clear we were supposed to pull over."

"Then I started thinking, If we stop now, they could do anything to us: kill us all, kidnap the children," explains Reg. "So I decided to accelerate, and I did."

But when Reg started to pull away, the bandits opened fire.

"It was terrifying," recalls Maggie. "First the back window was blown out and then Reg's window."

"I fixed my eyes on the road in front of me, and eventually they pulled away from me," says Reg.

"After the other car dropped back, it was such a relief. I looked in the backseat and I saw Eleanor and Nicholas still asleep," says Maggie. "We thought, Thank goodness they had slept through this."

"The feeling was great relief. We'd kind of done it, gotten away from them, and therefore it was the right decision to have taken," recalls Reg. "Well, we didn't know the full extent of the problem."

A few miles later, the Greens came upon a major traffic accident.

"By the side of the road there were police cars, an ambulance, and at first it seemed as if the policeman was telling us to go on," says Maggie. Reg pointed out the shattered windows to the policeman. "We managed to explain to them, you know, bang, bang, bang, men with guns, and what had happened," she says.

As Reg opened the back door to show the policeman more of the damage, he made a horrifying discovery.

"The interior light came on, and as it did, I saw this little patch of blood on Nicholas's head," he recalls.

"Nicholas! He's been hit! Help!" Maggie screamed.

"The policeman realized what had happened, and ran back to his police car shouting," says Reg.

"And then instantly, the ambulance was already there and they fumbled him out of the car and into the ambulance," adds Maggie.

"Nicholas had a little sheepskin that was now just a fragment of what it had been, but he slept with it virtually every night of his life," recalls Reg. "I said, 'He'll be frightened if he wakes up, unless he's got this with him.' They couldn't understand a word, but they could understand the mood."

"They took him away in an ambulance," says Maggie. "Men who didn't speak English took my little boy away, and that was a horrible feeling too.

"When we got to the hospital, they took us into a room, and put a chair out for me," she remembers. "And you know from the old movies that when they tell you to sit down, that's bad news."

"I have to be up front with you," the doctor told them.

"The chief surgeon simply said the bullet had struck the base of the skull where all the brain functions start from," recalls Reg. "They couldn't operate at that moment, and they only hoped that he would recover sufficiently for them to be able to operate."

"I will leave you to yourself for now," the doctor said. "I'm going to go back with Nicholas, but I want to promise you that we are doing the best that we can."

"So it was quite clear to us at that moment that this wonderful little brain that had been so forward, with bright dream and hopes, was going to be very severely damaged, whatever happened," admits Reg.

The Greens spent the next forty-eight hours waiting for news—any news—that their seven-year-old son was going to live.

"I will keep you informed if anything changes. I promise," said the doctor.

"I only got to spend a little time with Nicholas. That was very hard, too, not being able to see him," says Maggie. "He was in critical condition, and they wanted to do everything they could to protect him."

"Nicholas, Mommy and Daddy love you very much," she told him. "And you'll always be with us. And we'll always be with you."

"I wonder if they knew it was hopeless," Maggie says. "I

don't know. But I did get to hold his hand and talk to him. I got to tell him that I love him."

"They called us to the hospital after two days and sat us down again," says Reg. "All very silent."

"The result of the last test just came in," the doctor told them. "And there is still not any activity."

Nicholas was clinically dead.

"So Maggie and I sat there," recalls Reg. "We didn't say very much to each other. I remember holding hands and thinking, How was I going to get through the rest of my life without Nicholas."

"Now that he's gone, we should think about donating his organs," said Maggie.

"It was very simple for us to make that choice," she says. "There was this perfect little body that hadn't been harmed in any way, but the mind and spirit were all gone."

With that decision made, doctors prepared to use Nicholas's organs to give the miracle of life to seven young Italians.

"Nicholas's liver went to a woman who was nineteen years old, who was in her final coma that night. His two kidneys went to thirteen-year-old and eleven-year-old kids. His heart went to a fourteen-year-old who was no bigger than Nicholas, because he had been sick for so long," says Maggie.

"We met six of the seven all together with their families," adds Reg. "And to see this explosion of life, to think that one little body could do all this . . . yet it did. I mean, it saved all those families from going through the devastation that we were going through."

"Those organs aren't Nicholas's anymore," explains Maggie. "But that gift of living, and that generosity that was truly Nicholas's, is still giving. And another miracle here is that the girl who would have died, who received Nicholas's liver when she was in her final coma, has since gotten married and had a child. She's had a little boy who, of course, they've named Nicholas."

But the miracle didn't stop there. Reg and Maggie's decision to donate Nicholas's organs triggered an outpouring of love and gratitude from the entire nation of Italy. For their selfless generosity, the president of Italy presented them with a gold medal. Nicholas was revered as a national hero, and today his name can be seen on the walls of hospitals, schools, and memorials throughout the country. Since that fateful night years ago, the Greens have returned to Italy on dozens of occasions to honor their son and continue promoting the importance of organ donation.

"Organ donation rates in Italy have more than doubled after Nicholas died. And that means that, truly, thousands of people who would have died have survived today," states Reg.

Today, the Greens still keep in touch with the recipients of Nicholas's organs, as well as the many Italians who were touched by their generosity. Maggie and Reg have received countless gifts from the Italian people in Nicholas's memory. But none more touching than the bell tower that resides near their home in Bodega Bay.

"Bells started to arrived from all parts of Italy. And now there are 140 of them," says Reg. "The center piece was made by the foundry that's been making bells, the papers say, for the last thousand years. It's a magnificent bell, with

Nicholas's name and the names of the seven recipients. When the wind blows, you hear the bells ring, and when the wind picks up, you hear the whole orchestra play. A lot of us think that it sounds like happy children playing."

Reg recalls, "When we were on vacation right at the end, we played a game where Nicholas was a Roman soldier, and we were going to go back to Rome after many years of glory on the frontiers of Rome. We told him, 'There'd be poems written to you and children would cheer your name in the streets.' And everyone in Italy would know him.

"I mean, that was only a game, but it all came true. But the difference is that Nicholas conquered, not by the force of arms but by the power of love," says Reg. "And of course, that's much stronger."

# DIVINE INTERVENTION

# MEDICAL SCHOOL WINDFALL

"Kevin, do you know what you want to be when you grow up?" Nathan Stein asked his grandson.

"I don't know," Kevin replied.

"You don't know? Maybe you can consider becoming a doctor," Nathan said, "because that's what I wanted to be."

Sadly, Nathan Stein passed away in 1970, when Kevin was only ten years of age . . . never to know just how much he'd influenced his grandson's choice of career.

"I think my decision to go into medical school was ultimately made in my second or third year of college," Kevin Ladin explains. "I can recall my mother, in particular, expressing to me on a number of occasions that she wishes, or had wished, that my grandfather was around to see it."

Kevin was filling out medical school applications when his father joined him at the kitchen table.

"The challenge of paying for medical school was something that was on my mind," Kevin recalls.

"Dad, even if I do get into medical school . . . how am I going to even afford paying for the first year's tuition, it's fifteen thousand dollars alone?" Kevin asked.

Kevin's father, Sherman Ladin, refused to let fifteen thousand dollars spoil his son's plans.

"We'll find a way," he promised.

"I just felt that I would be able to send Kevin to medical school by just working a little bit harder," Sherman says, "and seeing that things would be taken care of."

Sherman was a real estate broker and decided to try to increase his sales. One morning, while reading the real estate section of the paper, he spotted an ad for a home for sale—by the owner.

"I contacted the owner and said, 'Hi. I saw your ad in the newspaper, and I'm just curious as to whether your house was still for sale. I realize you're trying to do this on your own. . . .' He was a little resistant about talking to me at first," Sherman admits. "He had been inundated with brokers calling him. I managed to keep him on the phone for about a half an hour, and at the end of our conversation, he said, 'You know, you sound like a nice fella. If I don't sell the house over the weekend . . . call me Monday.'"

On Monday, the home still wasn't sold, and Sherman arranged an appointment, which was later canceled.

"To make a long story short," Sherman explains, "we made ten appointments, and on the tenth appointment, I got another phone call to tell me that he was sorry, but he was unable to make that appointment at three-thirty that day. However, if I could come over now, he would meet with me."

When Sherman arrived at the house, he was in for an amazing surprise.

"I realized that this was the house that my in-laws owned before my father-in-law passed away," says Sherman. "I just couldn't believe that everything seemed to be much the same as it was when my in-laws lived there."

While Sherman was explaining the remarkable coincidence to the current owner, Mr. Toporov, there was a knock at the door. It was the postman, and he had a registered letter for Nathan Stein.

"Wait, that's my father-in-law," Sherman realized. "I'll sign for it."

"Well, I was absolutely flabbergasted," says Sherman. "I was in shock. Mr. Toporov couldn't believe what was going on."

"Well, go ahead and open it," Mr. Toporov insisted.

The registered letter was a final notice from a local bank, informing Nathan Stein that he had to claim a dormant savings account he'd opened nearly twenty years ago.

"The account was opened up for four thousand dollars," Sherman recalls his surprise, "and with interest over that period of years, there was over fifteen thousand dollars in there."

"The amount of money that was discovered in the bank account was almost the exact amount of my tuition for my first year at medical school," adds Kevin.

Nathan had opened the account in 1964, to help save

for Kevin's education . . . but after Nathan died, the account was forgotten.

"At the time my parents opened it up," Sandy Ladin says, "Kevin was the only grandchild. They had discussed his education and the thought that maybe it would be his dream to be a doctor as it was my father's. . . ."

"He made sure that Kevin was going to get those funds to take him into medical school. It was as if my father-in-law had conducted every phone call, every cancellation, until we were there at the right time at the right place," Sherman says. "We just couldn't believe it. I mean, it was just a miracle."

With the help of his grandfather's money, Kevin enrolled in medical school. And in 1998, he graduated as a doctor.

"I thought a lot about the coincidences that had to occur at the precise moment in time to allow for this to happen," Kevin reflects, "and I do believe there was some divine intervention that took place. I feel as though I fulfilled a dream of my grandfather's. . . . I believe he's still with me today. My empathy, my ability to communicate with other people, came from my grandfather. I feel, in a sense, he's been my guardian angel."

#  MESSAGE FROM TED

During his tour of duty in Vietnam, Army medic Nick Tassone saw his share of pain and suffering, and the images of death and despair followed him home. Like other returning soldiers, Nick tried to forget the horrors of war, but he had been forever changed.

Still, he and his wife started a family. And then in 1973, death and despair touched his life once again. His seven-year-old daughter, Dottie Marie, was struck down and killed by a speeding car. Her death would destroy his faith and his marriage, and leave him a lonely and bitter man. But Nick found a way back to life in a most unlikely place: a mental institution. It was here, working as a supervisor, that Nick learned that he had something left to give.

"I had the opportunity to help so many people get out of the hospital," says Nick. "I work with all the hard patients, because I just knew I had that gift. I could get them out of there if I could work with them. And I got so many different rewards from these people just leaving the hospital, saying 'thank you.'"

As Nick's heart opened to his patients, love found its way in, and, in February of 1992, he married Karen Webber. His youngest son from his first marriage, Ted, was their biggest supporter, and soon he moved into their home. Nick had a family once again.

Nick remembers, "Ted was my best friend. He was everything. We did everything together."

Karen adds, "Ted was compassionate toward other people. He was always willing to give a hand, or do anything for anybody at a moment's notice."

And then, on June 16, 1992, the unthinkable happened. Ted Tassone was involved in a head-on collision. His entire family rushed to U. Mass. Medical Center, where he was being operated on for head injuries.

Nick recalls, "They said the surgery is excellent, he is ninety-five percent, no problem at all. We just have to wait to see how he comes out of the twenty-four-hour period, and at eleven o'clock we could go upstairs to his room and talk with him."

But talking wasn't possible. Ted was being respirated through a tube in his throat.

"I asked him how he was doing. I told him to squeeze my hand for 'yes,' and squeeze my hand twice for 'no.' He was very alert. So the doctor said, 'Here's what we're going to do, Ted. We're going to sedate you now, and your father and mother will stay here. Tomorrow morning when you wake up, they'll be here.' "

Nick says, "I promised Ted that everything would be fine, and he was gonna be great. I never lied to Ted, so my word was my bond."

Later that night, Nick and Karen were trying to get some rest in a nearby room when they received some devastating news.

"A few hours later they called us to let us know that Ted's brain was swelling," remembers Karen. "The brain stem wasn't getting any oxygen, and no blood supply was coming through, and his brain was swelling out of control. And then at four o'clock, they said he was about ninety-eight percent brain-dead and that they didn't expect Ted to live too much longer."

His doctors gave him only a few hours to live, and suggested that the family stop the medication that was keeping Ted alive.

Karen explains, "If they continued with the medication that they were giving him to keep the brain functioning, it would have damaged the other organs. The other three kids and his ex-wife thought we should stop the medication in order to save his organs, because we were going to donate them. The doctor was there, and he said, 'You have to decide now.' "

Nick says, "I said no, I don't want to stop the medication."

The doctor told Nick, "Mr. Tassone, I know this is difficult for you, but this is the best thing for Teddy. Think of all the lives you're going to be helping because of this."

Karen recalls, "The doctor had told him if Ted had lived, he would be a vegetable—and we were going on the doctor's word."

And so, reluctantly, Nick signed the forms to discontinue life support.

"Then we were all allowed to see Ted," says Karen. "To tell him whatever you wanted to tell him before you left him, because after that, they were gonna stop the medication, and they were gonna operate to take the organs. So once you walked out of that room that was it, that was the last time you got to see him."

Nick remembers, "I said to Ted, 'I tried to let them keep you on the medication, but they voted against it.' I said, 'I love you and I'm sorry that I told you you were gonna live and you died.'"

Ted Tassone did not die in vain. His donated organs gave life to six other people. But that wasn't enough to console Ted's father.

Says Karen, "Nick literally was paralyzed with grief from the death of his son. In fact, he couldn't work. He would sit on the couch every morning in his bathrobe when I left for work. And when I came home in the afternoon, he would still be sitting there. He would write letters to Ted or he would tape messages into a little handheld recorder, to tell Ted how much he missed him and how much he loved him. And this went on for ten months."

Desperate and frustrated, Karen suggested that Nick join a prayer group. It was here that he would meet Father Paco, a man all too familiar with the loss of loved ones.

Nick recalls, "He gave me a little rundown of his life—how he lost his mother and father and sister in a car accident."

"I was devastated when my parents died," explains Father Paco. "In spite of being a priest, I was grieving. And Nick was grieving because he had lost two children. I said, 'Nick, you lost a son and I lost my father and mother. I could be your son and you could take the place of my father.' And he agreed. I thought it was a great idea."

Father Paco and the prayer group gave Nick the courage to return to work, but on one condition: that he wouldn't have to take any of his patients to U. Mass.

"It was always my job to take patients to U. Mass. for physical treatments. Well, after my son died at U. Mass, I didn't want to go there anymore. I just refused to go. I said, 'I just can't go there. I'm not ready to deal with this,'" says Nick.

He continued to stand firm until four years later, when he received an unexpected call.

"One day the telephone rang," Nick remembers. "And this lady says, 'I want you to pray for a girl at U. Mass. She was in a very serious car accident. They don't expect her to live.'"

Karen recalls, "Nick said to me, 'I just have a feeling that I need to go to U. Mass. and pray over this girl.'"

And so Nick contacted Father Paco and together they

drove to the hospital that Nick had vowed never to enter again.

"We were walking together, and I knew this was a very emotional thing for him," Father Paco remembers.

"Father Paco says, 'Let's go to the desk and find out where this girl is.' I said, 'Never mind, I know right where she is,'" recalls Nick. "So we went to the elevator, and went up to the fourth floor."

"When we got off the elevator, he said to me, 'This is the same floor where I was with my family when Ted died,'" says Father Paco.

"It was real, like déjà vu, you know. I didn't really stop to think of everything I went through with Ted. I just knew that when we got on the elevator and I put my foot on the floor, I had the cold sweats, but I knew that I had to do this."

The woman could be in any room on the floor, but Nick was pulled toward one in particular. When he entered that room, he was in for the shock of his life.

Father Paco remembers, "We started to walk to the room, and he said, 'This is the same room where Ted died.'"

"She was all taped up," explains Nick. "The only things you could see were her eyes and lips. And she said, 'Are you Nick? I have a message for you.'"

"We could see that she was in pain, and that she needed to rest," says Father Paco. "But her voice was actually excited."

The woman, Tais Morais, told them, "I went to a wonderful place. I know I wasn't here."

Father Paco says, "She said that she had actually died during the early hours of the accident."

It happened while medical personnel were frantically trying to save her life.

She told Nick and Father Paco, "All of a sudden, I saw my own self and I saw them working on my body. And I'm talking to them and I'm saying, 'Please don't worry about me, I'm fine.' "

The next thing Tais Morais remembered was being in a different world. And she wasn't alone.

"It was unbelievable. It was so beautiful. There were all kinds of angels, but they're all dressed the same. Everybody's in white. All of a sudden, I heard the voice of an angel say, 'Tais, if you decide to go back, tell my father I'm fine. Tell him not to worry.' And then all of a sudden, in the other room, I could see my whole family. I saw my oldest daughter crying, and I'm trying to say to her, 'Sandra, please,' I said, 'Mommy's okay.' Sandra said, 'I can't believe that you're going to die; I can't believe you're going to leave us. Please come back....' "

And with that, Tais began to return to her body.

"I knew the moment I made my decision. I knew it was going to be better. I knew nothing was going to be wrong with me—I had all that faith that I always did, but this time it was one hundred times more faith. I saw my self going back to my body. Then all of a sudden, these men were standing in my door. And I said, 'Nick, your son is in heaven. It's the most beautiful place in the whole world. And Ted said, "Tell my father I am fine." You can let go, Nick, he's in a good place. He loves you.' "

Father Paco remembers, "As she's telling this story, Nick and I are looking at each other. Nick is crying. So I got close to her and I was trying to comfort her as much as I could. But she was the one who comforted us."

"It was awesome," says Nick. "I don't think there is anything in the world that I could have heard that would have sounded any better at the time; it was so beautiful. And it was just the greatest feeling in the world."

"And from that moment on, Nick was able to, I would say, be totally healed," Father Paco says. "To let go of the pain and the frustration. He's not agonizing anymore about that. He's happy to know that his son is with God."

Eventually, Nick introduced his wife to the woman who changed his life.

Karen recalls, "He said, 'I need to take you to meet this girl, because you need to hear the story.' He said it's unbelievable."

Tais remembers that Karen told her, "Thank you, because Nick is a different person. You don't know what I went through with him when he lost his son."

"So I know my work was done," says Tais.

And the message she delivered healed Nick Tassone's broken heart.

"Ted was telling me to live for the living, not for the dead," says Nick. "He was saying, 'I'm all right, Dad. Go enjoy your life. And I'm happy. And thank you for being a good father.' That's what I read out of it. 'Thank you for being who you are.'"

# THE OTHER BOY

No one can predict when tragedy will strike—it can come at any moment. Kit Tucker of Kingston, Ontario, was about to discover this as she prepared for her three sons to arrive home from school. Kit always insisted the boys follow a daily routine.

"They would meet one another at the baseball diamond right outside the school," Kit explains. "When all three of them were together, they were instructed to walk home together because of safety factors and things like that."

But even this daily routine could not prevent the tragic accident that was about to happen. The three brothers were extremely close, although each of them had their own distinct personality.

"Ryan is quiet and tends to be studious," describes Kit. "Paul is a serious-minded boy. James was more high-spirited, not so much people-oriented as goal-oriented."

As the boys crossed the field toward home, James moved ahead of Ryan and Paul.

"Me and Ryan, my little brother, got into a small bickering argument," says Paul. "James decided he didn't want to hear it, so he just ran ahead."

As James ran toward the road, Paul suddenly realized the danger his brother was headed for.

"I could see out of the corner of my eye a van coming fast down the hill, right toward James, and I could almost tell it was going to hit him," recalls Paul.

"James, watch out!" Paul yelled, but James did not hear his brother's urgent scream in time, and the van struck him at over twenty-five miles per hour as he ran into the crosswalk.

"I ran over to him, and I felt that I needed to get him off the road before any other cars came," Paul says. "A woman came over and told me not to move him, not to pick him up, because he could have broken his back or something, and it would have paralyzed him."

Moments late, a Canadian military officer who served with James's father arrived on the scene. He recognized the boy and ran to alert his mother, shouting for someone to call 911.

Kit Tucker received the devastating news.

"I went to the front door," Kit remembers, "and a man burst through the door and said, 'Are you Mrs. Tucker?

Your son has been hit by a car.' I thought what every mother would think, Oh, my God! Who is it? How badly injured is he? Is he dead?"

Rushing to the scene, Kit still had no idea which of her sons had been struck by the vehicle.

"I was expecting it to be Ryan," Kit admits, "because Ryan was the youngest, and I would think that that was something the youngest one would do. I was surprised that it was James. I was filled with compassion when I looked at him and saw him lying on the ground. He was conscious at that point, and I spoke to him as soon as I saw him. I said, 'You're going to be all right, you're fine, Mommy's here. I love you, honey.' He was comforted by that."

Within minutes, paramedics arrived to tend to the injured boy. James's father, Len Tucker, had been summoned from the nearby army base.

"When I knelt down beside James," says Len, "my first feeling was anger. Who could do this? Why him? I think Kit took one look at me, and she could see that I was angry. She put her hand on my shoulder and said, 'He's okay. Everything's going to be okay.'"

James was rushed to a local hospital. The direct impact by the speeding vehicle would, almost certainly, have caused massive head injuries. But, miraculously, the only injuries that doctors could find were a few broken teeth.

"They had done X rays, they had tested him, and they couldn't really find anything wrong with him at all, except for his teeth. He needed to see a dentist," Kit says.

A few hours later, James was released from the hospital.

That night, with her son safely at home, Kit reflected on the incredible miracle that had happened that day: how her son had survived a major car impact with only a few broken teeth. Later, as she tucked Paul into bed, she discovered the miracle was even more incredible than she'd ever imagined.

"I was concerned about how they felt about the accident," says Kit. "And Paul said that he hadn't really been worried, because there had been another boy there, and he felt that he had been the one that was hit."

Paul's story about another boy being hit by the van seemed impossible, but she urged him to tell her exactly what he'd seen.

"I saw the van," Paul recounted, "and then I saw another boy, kinda translucent. He took the impact of the van. It protected James from getting injured on the side where the van hit him, and he got all his injuries from hitting the road, not from hitting the van. So the other boy protected him as his guardian angel."

"When Paul is talking to me," Kit continues, "he's a very straightforward child. He doesn't make up tales. Having been brought up with the idea of guardian angels, I think it clicked instantly. Something in me just said, This is a miracle. This is miraculous. This is something that is extraordinary."

"I believe the other boy was James's guardian angel," adds Paul, "and that God sent him to protect James from getting injured."

Today, the Tuckers spend their time enjoying their children, knowing that a miracle has enriched their lives. As for

James, he's fully recovered, thanks to the mysterious intervention of the other boy.

"I believe that the appearance of the other boy was a miracle," James states. "I think it was a miracle because I didn't sustain any injuries from the blow, I never had any broken bones, and I think that any other person without a guardian angel would have gotten a few injuries and broken bones."

Whether you believe in guardian angels or not, James is living proof that sometimes a tragedy can be miraculously prevented...although we may never know why.

# St. THERESA'S TWINS

Thirty-year-old Kristy Somerville had been trying to get pregnant for nearly a year when, one morning in October, she took yet another home pregnancy test.

"I remember looking at it and I screamed because I was so excited," she says.

She immediately woke her husband, Joe, with the incredible news.

"The most important thing in my life at that point was to have a child. Nothing else seemed to matter. I was just so focused on having a baby," says Kristy.

"I gave my wife a big hug right off the bat," recalls Joe. "I was just very excited, ecstatic."

A few weeks later, the Somervilles paid a visit to Kristy's obstetrician, and during a routine sonogram, he made an unexpected discovery.

"There are two embryos here," he told them.

"I didn't understand what he meant that he saw two embryos," says Kristy. "I thought maybe that was normal, because I had never been pregnant before."

She asked him, "Doctor, what do you mean by two embryos?"

"You're going to have twins," he said. "Congratulations!"

"We were excited about having one child, and now it's two," says Kristy. "I felt doubly blessed."

But a few weeks later, another examination brought them disturbing news: an additional ultrasound revealed only one embryo. Doctors had no explanation. The twin had vanished.

"We kind of had to readjust our thinking that we were gonna have twins," recalls Kristy. "Of course, we were still happy about having the one child, but we were really looking forward to having twins."

Three months later, having finally reconciled themselves to having only one child, Kristy had another sonogram.

"Hmmm . . . what's that?" asked Kristy, pointing to the sonogram screen.

"What do you think it is?" the nurse parried.

"It looks like another baby," said Kristy.

"Well, that's what you're seeing. There're two babies—there's one, there's two," replied the nurse, showing her the fetuses.

"I could not believe it," recalls Kristy. "I was on top of the world, knowing we were going to have twins again. I was just happy. I loved being pregnant. I had a spring in my step. I slept well. Things were looking good."

But Kristy's elation was cut short when, in her twenty-sixth week of pregnancy, she felt a pain in her abdomen.

"It felt like a cramp, you know, where it would tighten, then it just wouldn't go away," describes Kristy. "I knew something wasn't right. It just didn't feel right."

Kristy was going into labor. She was rushed to a hospital specializing in high-risk births in Grand Rapids, Michigan—three hours away.

"I prayed that my babies would be healthy," she says. "That they would stay inside the womb, warm and comfy, and that I could stay strong enough to have them make it to term."

Dr. Curtis Cook was in charge of Kristy's case.

"She was between six and seven months pregnant, and that's almost three months premature," he explains. "Babies can have a lot of complications if they're born that early. Some don't even survive if they're born that early."

Further examination revealed an even greater concern: An impaired umbilical cord was restricting the flow of blood to the smaller fetus, Baby "B." Without blood, the baby couldn't grow or develop. She was starving and suffocating at the same time.

"At that point, I was really scared," reveals Kristy. "And the first words out of the doctor's mouth were 'I don't think Baby B is going to make it through the weekend.' To have those feelings back again was really devastating."

"We felt it was very likely that the smaller baby was going to die in the uterus, and that it was too small for us to do anything about it at that time," admits Dr. Cook. "But our hope was to try to get the best outcome we could for the larger baby."

Kristy was immediately admitted to the hospital, where her early labor was stabilized. But doctors were unable to do anything to save the smaller twin.

"When you have this degree of abnormality in the umbilical cord flow, we have very limited options available," says Dr. Cook. "We don't have any medical therapies we can give her. We don't have any surgical procedures that we can do. All we can do is watch, wait . . . and hope."

"I had an overwhelming amount of guilt," says Kristy. "I felt that it was my fault. I thought that I had done something wrong. It was just a horrible place, emotionally, to be, especially knowing that a baby at one pound, five ounces is trying to fight for its life."

Meanwhile, her husband had booked a room at a nearby motel, in order to spend every possible moment with her.

"I just kept plowing the food into her," he says. "I just made Kristy eat more and more, just hoping that the baby would get some of that."

Kristy's mother, Cheri Johnston, kept watch over her as well.

"There was really nothing for us to do except pray," she says.

As devout Catholics, the family addressed their prayers to St. Theresa of Lisieux, "The Little Flower."

"St. Theresa died as a very young girl, and before her death, she promised that if God would allow her to intercede in any way, that she would bestow upon you a rose in an unusual manner," says Cheri.

"I asked St. Theresa to please open up Brigit's cord so that she would receive proper nourishment to grow and help her to survive," says Kristy. "I must've prayed for about an hour, saying those words over and over."

The next morning, Joe decided to take a new route on his walk to the hospital, and promptly became disoriented.

"I knew I was going in the right direction, but I didn't recognize the street I was on," Joe recalls.

Soon he came upon a church where a service was about to begin, and Joe decided to go inside.

"It was Palm Sunday," he says. "I sat through Mass, and then I spoke to someone who pointed me in the right direction toward the hospital."

On his way out, he picked up a sheaf of palms. When he arrived at the hospital, Joe showed the palm leaves to Kristy, and left them where she could see them.

"The palm leaves represent new life, and I thought that would give Kristy some hope," says Joe.

Later that afternoon, a local priest stopped by for a visit and noticed the palm leaves.

"Do you mind if I weave you something?" the priest asked.

"No, not at all," Cheri replied.

"He picked up the palms and he started to weave," recalls Kristy, "and I was thinking he was going to weave what everybody else weaves with a palm: a cross, of course."

"What are you weaving, Father?" asked Cheri.

"I'm weaving a rose," he said.

As Kristy and her mother watched, the priest's hands shaped the palm into something even more amazing—a double rose.

"Two roses for you," he said, handing it to Kristy.

"Thank you, Father," she said.

"You're welcome," replied the priest.

"Father, how many priests know how to weave roses like this?" Cheri asked him, and when he responded with "I believe I'm the only one," she said, "I think this is a sign."

Was this the sign they'd been waiting for? St. Theresa's rose was supposed to be an unusual one. And what could be more unusual than a double rose woven from the leaves of a palm?

"If this was a rose from St. Theresa, what it meant to us is that she was possibly going to intercede," says Cheri, "and perhaps there was a chance for the baby."

The next morning, everyone was amazed to find that the rosebuds had changed shape overnight.

"The rosebuds bloomed," says Kristy. "I definitely felt it was a sign. But there was still that little part of me that thought, This next ultrasound will be the true test."

The promise of the blooming rosebuds was fulfilled later that day.

As Kristy's doctor performed the ultrasound, he started to laugh, unable to believe what he saw.

The Somervilles were mystified, and Kristy asked him, "What is it, Doctor? What do you see?"

"It looks like the baby has grown," he revealed. "This

could be the best news we could have hoped for. She's going to get all the kinds of nutrients she needs."

"I'd never seen reversal in this type of a situation. Usually the babies die inside the uterus," says Dr. Cook. "I was quite surprised to see the baby doing well like that."

"Of course they're not going to say that it's a miracle, but at that point, I knew that St. Theresa had heard our prayers," Kristy asserts.

Four weeks later, Kristy gave birth to twin girls: two-pound, ten-ounce Maggie and one-pound, ten-ounce Brigit. At almost eleven months, Brigit and Maggie are typical babies for their age. And Joe and Kristy are extremely thankful.

"We couldn't ask for more. Both of them are very healthy," says Joe, adding, "Brigit and Maggie both had to fight for their lives inside the womb. I think outside the womb, they're going to be fighters their whole lives."

"I believe that it was a miracle that Brigit survived and that St. Theresa answered our prayer," says Kristy. "When you're in a situation where doctors are telling you that your babies are going to die, prayer is the one thing that keeps you going when there is nothing else. I believe that prayers are answered, and I believe that Brigit is living proof of that."

SECOND-CHANCE FAMILY

#  Mother and Child Reunion

In 1980, Kellie Robinson was just nineteen years old when she became pregnant out of wedlock. Realizing that she couldn't take care of the child on her own, Kellie made the difficult decision to have the baby and put it up for adoption.

"I wanted him to have a mother and father," she remembers, "and I wanted him to be able to have the things in life that I knew I couldn't provide at the time. It's just a hard thing to do, but for me, it was the right decision."

In the small town of Kanab, Utah, where she gave birth, Kellie wasn't even permitted to hold the beautiful baby boy she was giving away. And the aching desire to cradle him in her arms would haunt her year after year.

"I really wanted to hold him just one time to say good-bye, to tell him that I loved him, and why I was making the decision I was making. That opportunity was taken from me, and I'll never have it back again."

Eventually, Kellie met Thayne Forbes. They fell in love, married, and over the next ten years had three children, two girls and a boy. And then in 1992, a series of events would tear their lives apart.

"My husband and I went through a separation," Kellie says. "We went through a pretty rough year...and we got back together, but then there were a whole bunch of deaths that happened, including his grandmother, and then, six weeks later, my father."

During this emotionally devastating time, the Forbeses decided to sell their home and move into a larger one—doubling their mortgage. And almost immediately, they were hit with more bad news.

"My husband was laid off. And I did struggle to stay optimistic. I was still working, but three weeks later, I was also laid off and here we were in this new house....It was pretty devastating."

It was more than Kellie could bear. She fell into a deep depression. The only positive note in all this was that her layoff package offered career counseling. But when she called, the regular counselor was out of town. Because Kellie urgently needed to speak to someone, arrangements were made for her to meet with a substitute counselor. And so, on March 30, 1994, Kellie met with Shauna Bradley, a psychotherapist in private practice.

"I walked in and here was this woman who was blond and thin and beautiful, and I hated her for it. I guess maybe that's normal when you're depressed. But she put me at ease right away. She really did. During the counseling session, she asked me what I wanted to do with my life. One of the things I said was that I'd really like to write a book about my adoption experience. I just think it would be important to help someone else out there who has the same decision to make. And she started kind of getting a little teary and said, 'Adoption is a topic that is really close to my heart. I've been on the receiving end with my son, Jake.' She asked me if I had any regrets about it, and I said that I don't regret my decision, but the only thing I do regret was that I was not allowed to hold him."

"I asked her why she didn't get to hold him," Shauna remembers. "She said, 'It was Kanab, Utah. It was a small town.'"

Kellie says, "Her hands went up to her mouth and she said, 'Oh, my gosh, oh, my gosh.'"

Shauna says, "I could not breathe. It was like the breath had been knocked out of me."

In an unbelievable and miraculous twist of fate, Kellie was actually talking to the woman who had adopted her son.

"I was in shock," Shauna says. "How could this happen? Why is this happening? What am I gonna do?"

The chances of these two women ever meeting were phenomenal. They lived over sixty-five miles apart and hundreds of miles from Kanab.

"And I'll tell you," Kellie says, "it was like the weight of the world was lifted from my shoulders. He was in a home; I knew this was a good home."

The two mothers talked on into the evening, sharing their deepest feelings. Shauna gave Kellie a small photo of Jake Bradley, the son she had never known.

"It was really weird to look at it," Kellie says, "because it was a picture of a thirteen-year-old kid, and in my memory he was still an infant. It was just like the pages flipped and he grew up right in an instant for me."

Kellie learned that Jake had been a sweet and sensitive child, and that the Bradleys had two other children as well. Growing up in this warm and loving family, Jake had flourished. He loved the outdoors, camping and skiing, and enjoyed playing the saxophone...an instrument that both Kellie and her father had played.

The two women agreed to meet again, but Shauna felt that it was best to wait until Jake turned eighteen before telling him their incredible story.

"I totally understood," Kellie says. "I was just grateful for this much. Telling him was totally up to Shauna. I just asked her to give him a hug and a kiss for me when she got home that night. She promised she would."

But when they met for lunch a week later, Shauna had reconsidered and decided that it was better for Jake to learn the truth now rather than later.

"We didn't want him to feel like we were hiding things from him, or being secretive, 'cause we never had been that way with the adoption. We decided to tell him in this really casual way so it wasn't like this huge deal. One day, on a

Saturday after he got up, I said, 'You won't believe what happened to me the other day. I was in counseling and in walks this woman, and we discovered that she's your birth mother.' He asked what she looked like, and I showed him a picture. She looked just like him, and he was excited. He took the picture, went and showed his grandma and grandpa and all the cousins, everybody that lives around us; he had to show them all. It was fun."

A few days later, Kellie was waiting at a local restaurant to finally meet the son she'd given up those many years ago.

"I don't think I slept between the time I found out on Sunday and Tuesday, when we met," Kellie remembers. "And although I've had a chronic late problem in my life, I was thirty minutes early for that meeting. They kind of drove up to the side, we were standing out in front of the restaurant. It seemed to me that before the car even really got completely stopped, Jake jumped out of the car. And I looked at him, and I said, 'Oh, come here, I've got to give you a hug. I've waited so long for this.'"

Suddenly Kellie was holding her son in her arms, the one thing she'd wished for more than any other. And a lifetime of worry and regret melted away.

"I was really happy and excited," Jake says. "Nothing else in the world mattered to me at that time except that I knew that I had found her."

Inside the restaurant, Kellie and Jake began the long process of getting to know each other.

"So I asked him a bunch of questions," Kellie says, "and for about forty-five minutes, we just had a conversation.

But there was a point when it was appropriate for me to say, you know, 'Did your mom tell you what happened when you were born?' And he said, 'No.' And I told him that I had decided that I was going to place him for adoption because I wanted him to have things that I couldn't give him, and I said that even though I knew I was doing the right thing, it was still really hard. He put his hand out and took my hand and squeezed it, and it was as if he was saying to me, 'It's okay, I understand.'

"That was a pretty great gift he gave me, right there. Having gone through so many difficult things, feeling like life was just a misery, and then to have something so miraculous happen, and to have it happen at that point in my life, was just a life-changing event."

"I've always wanted to find out who my birth mother was," Jake says. "I truly think that it was a miracle. Or else I'd still be looking right now.

"It was a gift from God. I have no doubt about it. He lifted me out of the depths of despair."

# OLDER BROTHER

In 1942, nine-year-old Thora Knight was the only girl in her class in Leganier, Indiana, and the other twenty-three boys didn't make life easy for her.

"Being the new kid on the block, I guess all the boys had to prove themselves, as it were," she says. "They used to have a contest to see who could make me cry first, and whoever did won the contest for the day."

They would taunt her, saying things like "Do you have your lunch with you? 'Cause I'm getting really hungry."

"Please leave me alone," Thora would beg. "Why don't you pick on somebody your own size?"

"They'd tie my pigtails in knots. Anything to make me

cry. And when school was over, I went home and cried. I cried all the way home.

"I have very bad feelings about that school," recalls Thora. "It was a very lonely place for me."

Each night when Thora went to bed, she said a prayer, asking God to send a big brother to protect her.

"I began to imagine it," she says, "and the more I imagined this big brother, the more real he became to me."

And then one day, something strange happened.

"It's like someone walked up behind me and put their hand on my shoulder," remembers Thora, "but when I turned around, there wasn't anyone there. I just sort of said, 'Who are you?' and that's when I heard something that sounded like 'Jerriiee.' And when I first heard his name on the wind, from that point on, he was my big brother. He was Jerry, and he was right there."

The thought of having Jerry by her side gave Thora new confidence.

"I had this overwhelming sense of well-being, that it's okay," she recalls. "I had courage coming out of my ears."

The next time a bully approached her, saying, "Did you bring your homework for me to copy off of?" Thora responded, "You're not gonna get to do that anymore. Get out of my way!"

"You didn't hear me. You're gonna have to make me—" he said.

Thora pushed him away from her. "Get out of my way!"

"I whipped the socks off that little sucker," she laughs. "I did."

Thora's imaginary brother Jerry stayed by her side as she grew into a young woman, comforted by the sense of protection that he gave her.

By 1968, Thora's mother, Lillian, was living with her in Phoenix, Arizona. One evening Lillian received an unusual phone call.

"I heard her say, 'I didn't think you'd ever find me,'" recalls Thora, "and I thought it might be an old boyfriend. But the more she kept talking to this person on the phone, the more upset she became, and she started to cry. She hung up and she turned around and looked at me, and she was crying . . . and I looked and I knew."

"Oh, Thora," her mother said.

"Mom, do I have an older brother?" Thora asked her.

"Yes, yes, you do," Lillian admitted.

"I knew it. I knew it," Thora said, laughing. "I knew I had an older brother. Yes! Yes! Tell me everything," she said to Lillian. "You have to tell me everything."

"I don't know where to begin," said Lillian.

But Thora was in for an even bigger surprise.

"I found out his name was Jerry Hartman. Ah-ha. The voice on the wind all those years ago," she reveals.

Three weeks later, Jerry arrived from his home in Minnesota to be reunited with his birth mother and sister. Thora answered the door and gave Jerry a hug, and then Lillian joined in.

"That first hug is absolutely indescribable," says Thora. "I didn't want to let go. He was right where I could touch him and feel him and know he's real."

This new brother and sister spent the day learning about each other's lives.

"When I first met her, we'd talk for, I don't know, eight hours at a crack," says Jerry.

Jerry explained that he'd never known he was adopted until he became an adult and his parents revealed the truth: that his birth parents had been forced to give him up during the Great Depression. When he finally examined his adoption papers, he discovered their names: Lillian and Ralph Hawkins.

"It took quite a few years to locate Lillian," Jerry recalls. "We combed Indiana for Hawkinses, and we finally found one that knew them, and they said, 'Yeah, they're out in Phoenix.'"

"This is gonna sound strange," Thora said, telling Jerry about her school days, "but when I was a little girl, I imagined I had an older brother and he would protect me from all of the boys."

"If I had been there, you know I would've," Jerry told her.

"You try to make up for lost time, you know, but of course what's lost is lost," he says. "But to have a sister now, that's real nice. It's been more than thirty years since I met my sister, and now that I've had those thirty years with her, I feel like my life is complete."

"To have all of this suddenly come together," says Thora. "Mom has her son back, I have my brother... it's a miracle."

Jerry and Thora are no longer able to travel across the country to visit, but they keep in constant touch by phone.

"Even though we're miles apart, we're still together," declares Thora. "There's just that bonding there that even though I can't see him, or physically touch him, he will always be right here, right here. From the time I first felt that hand on my shoulder, it's always been there. And I know in my mind, my heart, that Jerry will always be right beside me."

# $\mathcal{L}$OST AND FOUND HOPE

In 1971, Theresa O'Konski was a single mother on welfare, raising a five-year-old daughter alone, when she gave birth to another child. Theresa made the painful decision to put the infant up for adoption: a healthy baby girl she'd named Hope Ann.

"I named her Hope Ann," explains Theresa, "in hopes that whoever adopted her would be good to her, in hopes that she would have a good future, and I hoped everything would work out for her."

But when she held the baby in her arms, she insisted on taking her home.

"I just couldn't let her go," Theresa says. "And so I

brought her home, and it was a struggle. I tried for three months. It was too much. They kept begging me to let her go and think of her and not myself. And so, finally, I did."

On the day the social workers came to take Hope Ann away, Theresa's five-year-old daughter, Doreen, watched as her mother's life fell apart.

Theresa protested, "I can't let her go. . . . I can't!"

But the social workers wouldn't give in. "No, I'm sorry," a social worker told Theresa, "you can't change your mind. . . . You've already promised. There is a couple waiting for her. They've waited for her for three months, and they're going to give her a wonderful home."

"It was just the worst day of my life," recalls Theresa. "If I could have died that day, I wouldn't have cared."

Doreen also remembers, "There she stood, broken-hearted, watching out the window, you know, watching her go away."

Twenty-seven years later, Theresa was facing another major loss in her life. Her seventy-seven-year-old mother was dying, and Theresa decided to move her into the nursing home where Doreen now worked.

"She was more sick than I thought she was," says Doreen. "I really didn't believe she was that ill, or that she was dying, but she was."

No one knew that moving her into the home would be the start of a miracle.

Conveniently, Doreen had made friends with a coworker, Beth Donnelly, who had been assigned to her grandmother's floor.

"I knew her on and off for about a year," Doreen remembers, laughing. "We seemed to hit it off really well. We had the same type of personality—outgoing, funny, joking."

Adds Beth, "We would just make each other laugh. She would crack me up. Actually, one time she had me laughing so hard I was on the floor."

The two women met daily to discuss Doreen's grandmother's condition. And although Beth was her charge nurse, Doreen would look in on her whenever possible. It was during one of these visits that something totally unexpected occurred.

"She saved pictures forever," Doreen explains. "I took the photo album out of her closet. . . . Beth came in, you know, dancing and joking, and she said, 'Let me see; I wanna see.' I didn't want to show her, because she'd say, 'Whoa, look at you, you were a fat little kid! You look silly.' I was afraid that she would make fun of me.

"She really wanted to see those pictures, so we went through the photos. We got to about the fifth page, and Beth asked, 'Who's that?' "

Doreen didn't know. "Babies . . . they all look the same," she said.

But Beth insisted, "What do you mean, you don't know? This is your family album."

"So," Doreen says, "I took it out of the photo album, and I flipped over the back of it. It read, 'Hope Ann, granddaughter.' My mother gave a baby up for adoption."

"Oh, my gosh," Beth exclaimed. "Hope Ann . . . oh, my gosh.

"I started crying," says Beth. "I said, 'That's me. I think that's me. I'm Hope Ann.' And she didn't believe me, actually."

Beth had been adopted in 1971 and knew that her birth name was Hope Ann. In an unbelievable turn of events, two friends had discovered that they were sisters.

"She just grabbed me," Beth recalls, "and gave me a big hug, and it just went on from there."

Beth suddenly realized that she had been taking care of her own biological grandmother, and she went to visit her now.

"I woke my grandmother up," says Beth, "and I said to her, 'I want to ask you something about your daughter, Terry. I was just wondering how many daughters she has.' And she said, 'She has one.' And I asked, 'No, can you really tell me how many she has?'"

"Oh . . . she had two . . . one was given up for adoption. It was supposed to be a secret," Beth's grandmother answered. "Hope Ann, I'll never forget her. I always wonder if she's okay, how she's doing, and how she made out in life. I hope she's having a wonderful life."

"And I said, 'She's okay, Gram. I'm her. I'm Hope Ann.' And her eyes literally bugged out of her head," Beth says. She and her grandmother hugged for the first time. "I couldn't believe it, you know? I was actually taking care of my grandmother."

As a final piece of confirmation, Beth realized she had seen the picture before. At home, she discovered her adoptive parents had the exact same photograph. Late that night, Theresa got a call.

"My daughter Doreen's husband called me," Theresa

says, "and I knew something was up, because he hardly ever calls me. And he said, 'You'd better brace yourself, Mom. I've got some news for you. You'll never guess who Doreen met.' And I'm naming all these stupid people, you know, I had no idea, and he said, 'Doreen found Hope Ann.'"

She continues, "And I said, 'What? What did you say?' And I dropped the phone and I started going through the house like I couldn't breathe. I couldn't sleep all night. I was all excited, and I was nervous and everything, and the next morning, I got a call."

It was Beth on the phone. "And she said, 'This is Beth...Beth Donnelly,'" Theresa says, "and she was stuttering, and she didn't know what to say, and I'm asking, 'Yeah, but who's Beth Donnelly?'"

"Um, I think I'm your daughter," Beth told her. "I'm Hope Ann. But I understand if you don't want to see me... I don't want to intrude."

But Theresa assured her, "Oh, darling...of course I want to see you. I want to see you right now."

They arranged to meet later that day at Doreen's home.

"I kept listening for the door," Theresa admits. "And then when the door opened, it was like my world opened again. My baby... I just looked at her, and that was my Hope Ann. I had her back. There's no question about it, she looked just like me."

"I just think it changed her life," Beth adds. "I think she feels wonderful. I know she loves me—I can tell. And I love her so much. And I think Grandma and God and everybody knew that we needed to be brought together."

A few days later, Beth visited her grandmother one last time.

"I went in there," explains Beth, "and I said, 'It's okay now. You can let go. It's time to go now. The family is all together.' I said, 'You don't have to suffer anymore.' And she said, 'I know.' She said, 'I want to die. I want to be with my mother.' And then, that night, she passed away."

Doreen continues, "I really felt strongly that she performed a miracle before she passed on. She just brought us all together."

"My grandmother's my angel," agrees Beth, "and I think she was sent from above. I really believe that."

"When Hope Ann came back into my life twenty-seven years later, it was the best day of my life, and I'll never ever forget it. I got a lot of making up to do, and I'm going to do it," Theresa concludes.

# MOTHER AND DAUGHTER REUNION

Tanya Fisher grew up in Winston-Salem, North Carolina, the only daughter of Fred and Hazel Smith. Her fondest memories are of playing with her younger brother while her parents worked hard to provide them a good home.

"They were strict but loving," recalls Tanya. "We would ride our bikes, but we weren't allowed to leave the yard."

But as Tanya grew older, she began to suspect that the Smiths weren't her biological parents.

"After I learned what adoption was, I asked my parents if I had been adopted," says Tanya. Hazel was dismayed, and told her that she never wanted to hear Tanya say that again.

"My mom said that my brother and I were their natural children, and that I should never speak of it again," she says. "A part of me wanted to believe her because she was, you know, my mother and she said it.

"But my mind just kept telling me . . . that's not so."

Despite her parents' denial, Tanya couldn't shake the feeling that she was adopted.

"In my heart I knew that this wasn't my biological family," she reveals. "So it was just a feeling of emptiness, like you don't belong to anybody. Because I didn't know who I was."

Tanya actually felt more at home with the woman who lived next door, Mrs. Trusdale.

"She was a grandmotherly type," Tanya says. "She was just a really nice lady. Whenever I saw her outside, I would go next door and sit on the step next to her, and we would just talk and laugh."

Mrs. Trusdale had a grown daughter who wasn't home much.

"Whenever I saw her daughter, she was just, like, in and out," Tanya explains. "She would speak to me, but it's not like she'd have a conversation with me."

"Mrs. Trusdale was the only adult friend that I had, you know, that I could talk to," recalls Tanya, and she was especially sad when her friend moved out of the neighborhood. "I hated that she was moving because I knew that I probably would never see her again," she says, even though Mrs. Trusdale gave her a big hug before leaving, and told Tanya to call her anytime.

Unfortunately, Tanya was right. The older woman passed

away several years later, without ever returning to see the little girl who loved her so dearly.

In the years that followed, Tanya grew into an attractive young woman, and in 1985 she married and moved away from the Smith household.

"I was looking forward to getting out on my own and being married and starting to have children," says Tanya. "A part of me was wondering about the children part, because I didn't know anything about my own background."

It wasn't until her father passed away that Tanya finally confirmed the nagging feeling that she was a stranger in her own family.

"I went over with my mom to sort out insurance papers and stuff," she recalls, "and while we were sorting through the papers, I came across my adoption papers. In my heart and my mind, I knew. But after I found those papers, it verified everything.

"I didn't know how I was going to find my birth mother, but I knew that some way, somehow, I'd try and do this," she states.

The adoption papers helped Tanya locate other records she hoped would lead her to her biological parents, but North Carolina's strict privacy laws kept that information secret.

"I did call the adoption agency that my parents went through to adopt me, but they couldn't help me. They just tell you that 'the records are sealed. We can't help you.' I just wanted to cry," she says. "It was really frustrating."

But Tanya refused to give up. She spent the next four

years desperately trying to convince someone to bend the rules, and reveal the identity of her birth mother. Finally, her persistence paid off.

She tried wheedling information out of a government clerk who held Tanya's papers, saying, "That is my real mother and I have a right to know who gave me my name."

The clerk told her once again that she was sorry, but she wasn't allowed to give that information out.

"She looked down at the paper and then she lifted it up," says Tanya, "and I saw the mother's name: Gwen Davis. Then she flipped it over, and I saw the mother's birth date. And I knew then that this must be my biological mother." Tanya was so excited by the discovery, she says, "If the clerk said anything to me after that, I didn't know."

Armed with this new information, Tanya learned that her birth mother worked for the city utility company. Anxiously, she placed a phone call, but didn't get very far at first.

"I really didn't know what to say, but I did ask to speak to her. She asked me who it was. And I just kind of hung up," admits Tanya. "I think I just felt good hearing her voice."

Tanya called her mother a second time, but once again hung up before identifying herself.

"I hung up because I got scared," Tanya says. "I was really feeling kind of childish by now, so I wrote down everything I was going to say, and I called her back."

Tanya jumped right in with the questions this time. "I think she was kind of confused," she remembers. "And so I said my name very slowly."

"How can I help you?" Gwen asked.

"That is my name, and I was given up for adoption on October 14, 1962," she replied.

"Tanya?" Gwen screamed. "It's my baby!"

"I was happy; I was excited," recalls Gwen of that phone call. "It was just unbelievable. After all these years, you know, and this child says, 'I'm your daughter.'"

"At first, when she screamed," says Tanya, "I didn't know if it was a happy scream or a mad scream."

"Are you mad at me?" Tanya asked.

"No. I could never be mad at you," said Gwen.

"When I gave her up for adoption, I really had no choice in the matter because I was just a child myself," reveals Gwen. "So, when she was born, I saw her maybe for about five minutes. And that was the last I saw of her."

The two women agreed to meet that afternoon at Gwen's office. Tanya waited anxiously in the lobby for her mother to appear.

"When she came out, we just kinda looked at each other," remembers Tanya. "I knew that that was my mother. I looked just like her. For the first time, I felt that I belonged to someone," she says. "She held her hands out for me to come to her, and we just hugged."

"It was scary, but it was exciting," says Gwen. "I felt something inside that was just really unbelievable."

"It really felt good, you know, because to me, this was my mother," says Tanya. "This was my mother."

That night, Tanya visited Gwen at her home, where they continued to get to know one another.

"I told her that I had grown up on East Twenty-fourth Street," says Tanya. "And then she said, 'I lived on East Twenty-fourth Street too.' As soon as she said it, I said, 'Mrs. Trusdale was your mother. Gwen, we were neighbors. We were neighbors!'"

It turned out that Gwen was the seldom-seen daughter of Tanya's old friend and neighbor.

"I had watched her for so many years, just playing and then sitting on our front porch," recalls Gwen. "We saw each other, but we did not know that we had that sort of relationship: mother and daughter."

Which meant that Mrs. Trusdale, Tanya's only adult friend as she was growing up, was her grandmother.

"There was just something about that little girl next door," declares Gwen. "My mother and her would always be laughing and talking with each other."

"I think maybe this was God's way of my grandmother seeing me," says Tanya, "because she had died before Gwen and I were reunited."

Gwen adds, "I think my mother knows. Even today she knows, and I think she's very happy."

Today, Gwen and Tanya are as close as any mother and daughter can be.

"I love her with all my heart," says Gwen. "Sometimes I can be down, and I can talk to her and things just brighten up for me."

"I believe in prayer and mine was answered," says Tanya. "I always wanted to know who my real mother was, and I got that through prayer."

"I prayed for Tanya too," Gwen concurs. "I just asked the Lord if maybe one day he would let me see her again, and in due time, he brought her back into my life. It took a lot of years for my prayers to be answered, but they were answered." She adds, "It's a miracle, and it's a blessing, because that's something that just doesn't happen every day."

# WRONG-NUMBER MIRACLE

In June of 1999, after the sudden death of her husband, Evelyn Trant contacted her friends and family with the news. But there were two longtime friends she couldn't locate.

"Well, I just happen to think that we need to get in touch with Ronnie and Johnny Godsey," Evelyn said. "You know they'll want to know."

Evelyn's daughter-in-law, Caren, offered to help.

"I'll find them," she told Evelyn. "Don't you worry about a thing. I'll go do it right now."

"So we just called Directory Assistance," Caren recalls, "and asked if they had a number for Godsey, Ronnie or Johnny. I figured one could get hold of the other."

But there were no listings available for a Godsey with either first name.

"Well, do you have anything with an 'R' or a 'J' or maybe a middle initial?" Caren tried asking the operator.

"She explained to me that she had a million Godseys, and that I couldn't just narrow it down by using somebody's middle initial," says Caren. "I said, 'Well, pick somebody who looks related to them'—like she would know who was related to somebody."

"Well, then, could you give me two names, please?" Caren then asked.

"She gave me a David Godsey out of New Orleans, and she gave me an Eric Godsey out of Lake Charles; I guess assuming that we might find somebody related in a different area."

Caren called the first number and reached David Godsey in Houma, Louisiana.

"My wife and I were watching TV, and the phone rang," recalls David Godsey, Sr. "And this lady told me she was looking for a Ronnie or a Johnny Godsey."

"No, I'm sorry, I don't know anybody by that name," he told her, "but I can help you out."

"He didn't know them, but he was telling me how you look for somebody on the Internet," recalls Caren.

"Yeah, I've had a lot of practice," he said.

"He had lost track of his son," she says. "He'd been looking for him for twenty-six or twenty-seven years."

"You've been looking for your son for twenty-six years? Wow," said Caren.

"I'm very good on computers, that's why I've been working the Internet lately," David senior told her.

"When David was two, his mother and I, we had some disagreements, and we just couldn't live together anymore," explained David senior. "So we decided the best thing would be for us to separate, for the children. She moved back to California, and then I lost track. And once I lost track of them, that was it."

David kept trying to find his missing son, but a personal tragedy pushed him to step up the search.

"I had an older son," says David senior, "and he was killed in 1989. That was a great loss to me, and it made me want to find David even more. So that's when I really started looking harder for David."

But after several years, it seemed like his son had vanished from the face of the earth.

"It was just heartwrenching," says Caren, "because you're going, Gosh, here's this guy looking for somebody all this time. He wished me luck, and I wished him luck. And I got off the phone and decided to call the next person on the phone list, which was Eric Godsey."

"We were just sitting there trying to figure out what to do, when the phone rang," recalls David Godsey, Jr. "My wife went into the hallway to talk to whoever was on the phone. I didn't get to hear too much of it, but when she came back into the hallway, what I heard her saying was 'Let me let you talk to my husband.'"

"She put her husband on the phone," says Caren. "He suggested that he didn't know his family," she says. "He'd never known his father because they'd lost track when he was little."

"I haven't seen my father since I was two years old and I don't know anyone on that side of my family," David junior told her.

"When he was saying those things, I just got chills. It was kind of like, Whoa, you know?" says Caren.

"She said, 'Well, you know, I just got off the phone with a man who hasn't seen his son since he was two. He says his name is David Godsey,' " recalls David junior.

He explained to Caren that he had spent many years during his childhood searching for his father.

"Whenever I was younger and my mom used to travel up to see my grandmother in New Hampshire, everywhere we stopped I always looked in the phone book to see if I could find any Godseys," David junior remembers.

But he ended his search after receiving some devastating news.

"Back when I was about sixteen years old, there was a plane crash up in Washington State, I believe, that killed a bunch of military personnel," says David junior. "They had printed the passenger list in the newspaper, and on the list there was a man named David L. Godsey. That's my father's name: David Louis Godsey. My mom had seen it and she pointed it out to me. And it just really was kind of heart-breaking."

"You know, what if I give you this person's phone number—would you please call him? I'll give you my number and you can call me back. I just have the strangest feeling.... I really think this could be your dad," asserted Caren.

"Why are you doing this?" David junior asked her.

"With the alarm in the son's voice, I was afraid that he would not call his father," says Caren. "And we didn't want to lose this. We felt like we had something."

"I think this is great," she told him. "I can't believe it."

And so Caren called David Godsey Sr. again, only to receive some sobering news.

"No. No, I'm sure that's not him," David senior told her. "I'm sure of it. His name is not Eric. It's David Edmond."

The facts seemed to match, but the names didn't.

"The listing I had for the phone number was in Eric Godsey's name," says Caren. "Maybe he decided to change his name?" she said to David senior. "Maybe he didn't like Edmond. I don't know if I would like Edmond."

While they were talking, the young man in Lake Charles gathered up his courage and called the number he'd been given.

"I got an answering machine, so I left a message," says David junior.

"I'm trying to reach a David Godsey. Um...this is concerning your son. Could you please return my call."

At the same moment, Caren was busy convincing David senior to call the number in Lake Charles.

"No, I'm sure that's not him," David senior declared.

"He said his son did not live in Louisiana, because the last he knew, his son was in California," recalls Caren.

But he finally agreed to call.

"Well, I'll try it, you know, since you've gone to the trouble," he told Caren.

"Okay," she said. "Here's his number, but then can you call me back and let me know if it is him?"

David senior agreed, and thanked her. "After I got off the phone with Caren, I listened to his message," says David senior. "So I called him up."

"This is David Godsey. I received a message on my answering machine saying you might have some information on my son?" he said.

"Well, yes, sir," responded David junior.

"Have you been talking to Miss Caren?" David senior asked.

"Uh, yes, sir," said David junior.

"Well, my son's name is David, not Eric."

"No, no, no, no, no. My *son's* name is Eric. I'm David."

"Where you from?" asked David senior.

"I'm from California."

"California. That's where my son's from. Okay, let me ask you a question: Do you have two sisters?"

"Yes, I do."

"One named Wendy and one named Sandy?" asked David senior.

"Yes," said David junior. "He said, 'Uh, well, hello, son. This is your dad.' "

"And we were both so . . . we couldn't think of anything to say," recalls David senior.

"It was just wonderful," says David junior. "It just filled

something in my life, you know? Knowing that I do have a dad. And knowing that he wants to know me."

Meanwhile, Caren and her family were anxiously awaiting the news. When the phone rang, Caren picked it up, asking, "Hello? Is it him?"

"Yes, it is him," responded David senior. "It's him. I can't believe it."

"Hold on one second," she said. "It's him!" she told her family, who greeted the news with screams of joy. "We were yelling, 'It's the father,' 'It's the son,' you know, 'They're related,' and I was yelling, 'The phone's listed in the grandchild's name.' Can you believe it?

"I am so happy for you," Caren told David senior.

"She was tickled to death that she had been a part of being able to help bring two people back together after so many years," says David senior. "And she said, 'I watch TV programs or see on the news where people find a long-lost relative that lives fifty miles away from them and they never knew it, but I never thought I'd be a part of something like that.'"

On July 4, 1999, father and son were reunited for the first time in twenty-six years.

"We just walked up toward each other and gave each other a big old hug," recalls David junior. "How you been?" he asked his father.

"I've been looking all over for you," his father responded.

"One of the amazing things about it," remembers David senior, "was that I was dressed in a checkered shirt with jeans and cowboy boots, and he was wearing almost exactly the same thing. And we didn't know what we were going to be wearing.

"And he looks so much like me," David senior adds.

While David and his father continue to spend every available moment together that they can, neither of them had ever met the woman who had brought them together. And so, *It's a Miracle* arranged for them to finally meet.

"It's just a miracle that we were brought together," says David senior. "We may have not ever found each other if it hadn't been for Caren Trant."

"They keep telling me thank you and I'm going, 'I didn't do it.' I could not have done this intentionally," says Caren. "Obviously, I couldn't find Ronnie and Johnny, and that's who I was looking for."

"You guys look alike," she told them when they finally met.

"Yeah, you don't know how much we are alike," said David senior.

"Everybody has their job and you get through your daily life and you don't know that you affect other people. But you affect other people every day," says Caren. "The operator, she will never know that she got a father and son together that had been looking for each other. She'll never know that that wasn't just an everyday event in the life of an operator, one more phone number that she gave out.

"To me, it is a miracle. Because you couldn't do it on purpose. We couldn't have made the connection. It had to have a bigger hand."

"Caren was a godsend," declares David senior. "There had to be a reason for her to call me, and for her to call David, and for us to get together like we did.

"I don't know what to say other than it was a miracle. That's the only thing I can come up with."

# About the Author

RICHARD THOMAS is a highly respected actor who reliably inspires audiences with his versatility. He went professional at age seven, stepping onto the Broadway stage as a young John Roosevelt in *Sunrise at Campobello*. His feature film debut came at sixteen in Universal Studios's *Winning*, starring Paul Newman and Joanne Woodward.

But Thomas stole America's heart with his sensitive portrayal of John-Boy on *The Waltons*, a role that won him a Best Actor Emmy and catapulted him into the spotlight at twenty-one. Since then, he has consistently aligned himself with quality projects, starring in over thirty-eight movies for television, including such classics as *Roots, All Quiet on the Western Front, The Red Badge of Courage, The Homecoming, The Christmas Box,* and many others. His most recent appearance on the big screen was in Paramount Pictures's *Wonder Boys*.

Along with his television work, Thomas is a critically acclaimed star of the theater, having revealed himself over the years to be equally at home in the classics and modern masterpieces. He most recently completed a run on the London Stage in the West End production of *Art*.

The actor has taught at universities on behalf of the Kennedy Center's educational programs, served as the National Chairman of The Better Hearing Institute and on the board of The Morris Animal Foundation, and has been honored with a doctor of fine arts degree from the University of South Carolina. He also serves on the board of the Center Theater Group, his theatrical home in Los Angeles.

For his passionate performances, charged with emotional authenticity, Richard Thomas undeniably has become one of America's most revered and beloved talents. As host of *It's a Miracle,* he brings tremendous compassion and joy to chronicling true-life accounts of miraculous events and divine interventions.

He lives in Los Angeles with his wife, Georgiana, and their children.

Submit your own

IRACLE

to the producers of
PAX TV *It's a Miracle* at:

Submit Your Miracle
c/o Executive Producer
*It's a Miracle*
10880 Wilshire Boulevard
Suite 1200
Los Angeles, CA 90024

Or please visit the *It's a Miracle*
website at *www.itsamiracle.tv*

# IF YOU LIKE THE STORIES IN THIS BOOK, TUNE IN TO PAX TV.

Every week you'll enjoy heartwarming characters, uplifting stories, exciting dramas and original movies. Check your local listings and enjoy our family friendly brand of television today.